Smart Guide to
the Internet

Stephen L. Nelson

BARNES
&NOBLE
B O O K S
N E W   Y O R K

D1372067

Copyright © 1999 by Stephen L. Nelson, Inc.

This edition published by Barnes & Noble, Inc., by arrangement with Stephen L. Nelson, Inc.

1999 Barnes & Noble Books

ISBN 0-7607-1912-8

Printed and bound in the United States of America

01 02 MP 9 8 7 6 5 4 3

QWF

CONTENTS

CHAPTER 6 Using E-Mail   **97**

CHAPTER 7 Working with Newsgroups   **125**

INTRODUCTION

None of us wants to linger in a book's Introduction. We want to get on with it, begin reading the important stuff, and begin getting answers to questions. Nevertheless, let me suggest that you take time to read or at least skim this Introduction. It briefly discusses the following important topics so that you can get the most out of this book:

- How to use this Smart Guide
- How this book is organized
- Assumptions about you
- Conventions used here

How to Use This Smart Guide

If you're brand new to the Internet and want to learn everything you can in as short a time as possible, then you should read this book from start to finish. But if you've worked with the Internet a little in the past, you might want to skip around in the book. You might not need to read Chapters 1 and 2, for example. Instead, you might want to begin with Chapter 3 and read to the end, or read only those chapters that describe the tasks you want to accomplish.

You can also use this book as a reference for those times when you're puzzled about how to work with a feature. Just turn to the table of contents or the index to look up the topic that's causing you trouble. Then you can dip right in, read a few paragraphs to answer your questions, and get back to work. This book is written in a way that allows you to read it using all of these techniques.

How This Book Is Organized

The *Smart Guide to the Internet* has ten chapters and a Glossary:

Chapter 1, "A Brief Introduction to the Internet," describes what the Internet is, where it came from, how it works, and the many things you can do on it.

Chapter 2, "Connecting to the Internet," describes everything you need to connect to the Internet and presents different connection options. It also details how to set up a connection.

Chapter 3, "World Wide Web Basics," talks about what you can expect to find on the World Wide Web and how you navigate the Web using the two most popular Web-browsing software programs.

Chapter 4, "Finding Information," describes tools you can use to sift through the volumes of information available on the World Wide Web.

Chapter 5, "Popular Places to Visit on the Web," is a listing of places you might want to check out as you begin your Web browsing.

Chapter 6, "Using E-Mail," describes what e-mail is, explains how it works, and shows you how to use two popular e-mail programs.

Chapter 7, "Working with Newsgroups," tells what newsgroups are, explains how they work, and shows you how to use the e-mail programs described in Chapter 6 for browsing newsgroups.

Chapter 8, "Chatting Online," describes how you can use special Internet software for communicating with others in real time.

Chapter 9, "The Rest of the Net," describes some Internet activities that you might want to pursue.

Chapter 10, "A Web-Publishing Primer," details how you can create your own presence on the World Wide Web.

The Glossary defines terms related to the Internet that you are likely to encounter.

Assumptions About You

As I wrote this book, I had to make a few assumptions about your computer skills and knowledge. I tried to make this book apply to the widest range of people and experiences as possible. However, people use different programs, have different Internet setups, and possess varying degrees of knowledge about computers. In a little book such as this one, there's just not room to describe all the different ways that you can make use of the Internet.

This book assumes that you have either Microsoft Windows 95 or Windows 98, and that you'll be using one of the two most popular free suites of Internet software, Microsoft Internet Explorer or Netscape Communicator.

Chapter 2 describes the various Internet software programs that are available and what you can do with each of the above-mentioned suites.

Although this book introduces computing terminology and steps you through some complex tasks, it is designed to be useful to people who have never before worked with the Internet using Internet Explorer or Netscape Communicator. If you're a beginner, you'll find it helpful to know some Windows basics before you begin reading. For example, you should know how to start and stop programs, choose commands, and work with dialog boxes. If you need to learn these skills, you might want to look for the *Smart Guide to Windows 98*.

Conventions Used Here

This book uses some simple conventions for presenting information. When I want to share a tidbit of information that is relative to the topic at hand but interrupts the flow of discussion, I'll set that information apart with an icon in the margin.

 A Note provides backup or additional information that relates to the general discussion but isn't critical to your understanding. A Note is also used to point out exceptions for special situations.

 A Tip offers advice or presents information that can save you time and trouble.

 A Warning alerts you to potential trouble spots or mistakes easily made.

From here on out, whenever you see a **boldface** term, it means that term is defined in the Glossary. A Glossary term is set in boldface the first time it's used in a chapter. For example, if the term **modem** is used in a discussion and you don't know what a modem is, you can flip to the Glossary in the back of the book and look it up.

CHAPTER 1

A Brief Introduction
to the Internet

The **Internet**—it's all the rage. But what's it really all about? Why would anyone want to get connected? This chapter addresses those questions by covering the following topics:

- What is the Internet?
- How the Internet works
- Safety, privacy, and content concerns

What Is the Internet?

In short, the Internet is a group of *inter*connected *net*works. When you hook up with a company such as America Online, you're connecting your computer to the Internet through one of these **networks.** In other words, the Internet is a worldwide group of millions of connected computers, people, and software programs that work together to share vast quantities of information. The number of people who use the Internet doubles in size about every six months. People enjoy the Internet because it's an inexpensive, efficient, and entertaining way of communicating. And because of the Internet's popularity, it keeps getting bigger as more and more people join in.

The Internet goes by many names: "the Net" is a popular nickname, and the novelist William Gibson coined the term *cyberspace.* Perhaps the most descriptive name for the Internet is the "Information Superhighway." Indeed, the Internet is much like a worldwide highway system—thousands of people enter from different on-ramps at any given moment, and, by means of different types of vehicles, each person then heads off in a different direction to one of millions of possible destinations.

The Internet consists of several parts that you can use to accomplish different tasks. Table 1-1 outlines some of the most popular methods for sharing information and what you can do using each method.

Internet Part	How You Can Use It
E-Mail	Send and receive messages and files. As with regular mail, you can send individual personal messages to people, and you can also send and receive mass mailings. Chapter 6 describes how to use **Microsoft Outlook Express** and **Netscape Messenger** for **e-mail.**
Newsgroups	Post and read messages on electronic bulletin boards for people with a common interest to share. Chapter 7 describes how to use Outlook Express and Netscape Messenger for reading and posting **newsgroup** messages.
World Wide Web	View information in the form of colorful, multimedia documents that businesses and individuals publish for people to see. Or publish your own information for others to see. Listen to radio stations and view videos broadcast over the Internet. Send and receive free web-based e-mail. **Download** files to save on your computer, such as free software. Chapters 3, 4, and 5 describe some of the neat things you can do on the **World Wide Web**. Chapter 10 describes how you can publish your own information on the Web.
FTP	Post files for other people to download or download copies of files that other people have posted. Chapter 9 describes working with File Transfer Protocol **(FTP)** sites.
Telnet	Connect to places such as your local library or a **server** at your place of work. Chapter 9 describes the basics of using **Telnet.**
Chat Rooms	Communicate with others in real time, either by typing back and forth or by sending audio and even video. Chapter 8 describes chatting online.

TABLE 1-1: What you can do in some of the most popular parts of the Internet.

How the Internet Works

The many different parts of the Internet work in numerous ways, but they all use the same network of computers and transmit information in the same way.

 The term network refers to any number of computers connected together.

To take the Information Superhighway metaphor a bit further, the beauty of the Internet is that if construction is slowing down traffic on one road, the information that you want can get to you via another road. It just might take a little longer. When you connect to the Internet, you are constantly sending and receiving information. This information is broken down into pieces called packets. Every packet is labeled in sequence (1, 2, 3, 4, etc.), so if one gets lost, the computers know to try again.

 Ever wonder where the Internet came from? The Advanced Research Projects Agency (ARPA) of the U.S. Department of Defense developed it in the 1960s for defense-related research. The ARPANET, which evolved into the Internet, was also specifically designed to outlast other means of communication during a nuclear attack. The ARPANET network was special because it connected key communication centers with several different routes. It is this "redundancy" that makes the Internet as reliable as it is today.

Safety, Privacy, and Content Concerns

Although the Internet might sound appealing to you, you might still be hesitant to connect if you've caught wind of some of the safety, privacy, and content issues that the Internet raises.

How Safe Is the Internet for Shopping?

Shopping on the Internet has its obvious benefits: it's always open, you don't have to leave the comfort of your own home, you can easily purchase products from around the world that may not be readily available in your community, and it's often a great place for bargains.

So if you're a savvy consumer, the idea of shopping on the Internet probably sounds interesting to you. However, you may also be hesitant about sending people your credit card and mailing information over the computer.

Internet shopping is not inherently more dangerous than any other type of shopping in which you use a credit card. Just as when you shop at a local store with your credit card, a devious person can find a way to get hold of your account number and expiration date and charge purchases to your account. But the technology behind Internet shopping in and of itself is not unsafe. Newer Internet software programs have several safety features you can implement to take advantage of the most up-to-date advances in technology. And it's worth noting that when you shop at a local business with a credit card, that business sends your credit card account and purchase information *electronically* to the credit card company to bill you for the purchase. However, in addition to taking regular precautions with your credit card information, there are steps you can take to make shopping on the Internet a safer experience.

- Send credit card and other information only over a secure, encrypted connection.

Most **web sites** scramble or encrypt information like credit card numbers to ensure the safety of personal data. As you enter a secure site, your **web browser** by default alerts you to this fact by displaying messages similar to those shown in Figures 1-1A and 1-1B.

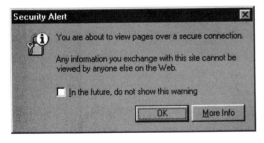

FIGURE 1-1A

The message that Internet Explorer displays as you enter a secure web site.

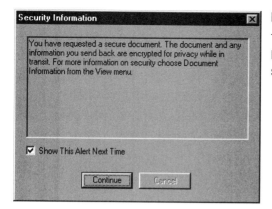

FIGURE 1-1B

The message that Netscape Navigator displays as you enter a secure web site.

 If you look at the Address or Location box of your web browser, you can see that the line begins with the letters "https." The "s" signifies that the site is secure.

To verify the security of a web site with **Netscape Navigator,** click the Security toolbar button to display the Security Info window shown in Figure 1-2.

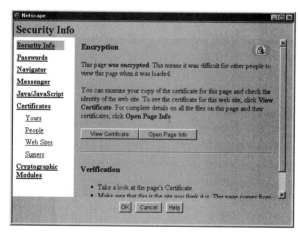

FIGURE 1-2

Security information for a secure web page at barnesandnoble.com.

To tell Internet Explorer to notify you as you enter or leave a secure site, start Internet Explorer and choose the Tools menu's Internet Options command. Click the Advanced tab, and then scroll down and select the Warn If Changing Between Secure And Not Secure Mode check box, as shown in Figure 1-3.

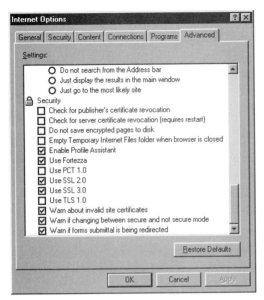

FIGURE 1-3

Setting security options in Internet Explorer.

It's wise to allow your browser to notify you every time you enter or leave a secure web site or send information over an unencrypted connection. To tell Netscape Navigator to do this, follow these steps:

1 Start Netscape Navigator, and click the Security toolbar button.

2 Select Navigator from the list on the left to display the options shown in Figure 1-4.

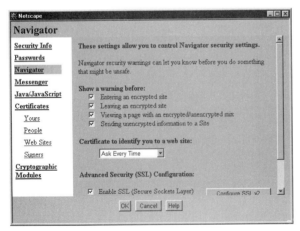

FIGURE 1-4

Setting security options in Netscape Navigator.

3 Select the Entering An Encrypted Site, Leaving An Encrypted Site, and Sending Unencrypted Information To A Site check boxes. Because some web sites include a mix of data from secure and insecure sites, you might also want to select the Viewing A Page With An Encrypted/Unencrypted Mix check box.

• Be sure that you're sending the information to the party you think you are.

On the Internet, it's easy to pretend to be someone you're not. If you have reason to doubt that a party is who he or she purports to be, verify the source of the web site before you send your personal information. You can verify sources of web sites by checking the web site's certificate. A **certificate** is a form of documentation issued by a third party that vouches for the identity of the company. To view a certificate in Internet Explorer, choose the File menu's Properties command and click Certificates. Using a certificate like the ones shown in Figures 1-5A and 1-5B, you can verify the source of the **web page.** In Netscape Navigator, click View Certificate to display the company's certificate.

FIGURE 1-5A

Certificates as displayed by Internet Explorer allow you to verify a web page's source.

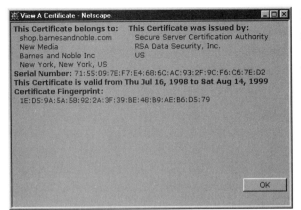

- Do not give your credit card information to companies whose reputation or trustworthiness you question.

Although the Internet can be a great place for bargains, it can also be a great place for con artists. Think twice before you give out your personal information, such as your credit card number, to a company you don't recognize or one whose reputation you're unsure of. Remember that if a deal seems too good to be true, there's probably a hitch, so ask for a printed catalog or call the company for information. Also, be sure to ask about the company's return policies.

- Use only credit cards, never debit cards.

If you notice unauthorized transactions on a credit card account, you can notify the company and have the transactions investigated and reversed. With debit cards, on the other hand, a thief can quickly empty your bank account and leave you with no funds and no legal recourse.

Keeping Your Personal Information Private

If you're uncomfortable with the trend of more and more businesses nowadays wanting to know everything about you—your address, telephone number, e-mail address, household income, shopping habits, Social Security number, and so on—you also need to protect this information when you're on the Internet. Here are some tips for keeping your personal information private.

- Guard your password, even from people claiming to work for your Internet service provider (ISP).

If you give out your password, a malicious person could run up your account fees or change your account options. The people who work for your ISP should never request your password. If they do, refuse the request and report the incident to your ISP immediately.

- Be careful about giving out your phone number and home address on the Internet.

Part of the fun of the Internet is its anonymity—it allows people to go beyond appearances and overcome inhibitions. But this can also be dangerous. The people you meet aren't always who they claim to be. You may want to use an **online** alias. If you want to meet someone you've gotten acquainted with online, agree to meet in a safe public place, perhaps accompanied by a friend or relative. The rules that you should follow for meeting someone you chatted with online are no different from those you should use when meeting someone new through a personal ad in a newspaper. Be careful.

- Before giving a company on the Internet your personal information, look for a privacy policy that describes ownership and usage rights of the personal information you submit, and whether this information can be provided to third parties.

Many companies request that you register and submit personal information before you can make full use of their web sites. A company that is sensitive to privacy issues will post its privacy statement prominently on its web site and offer you options about the use of your personal information (see Figure 1-6). You should be able to choose whether or not you want the company to use the information you submit.

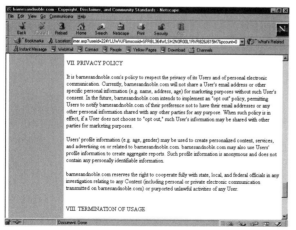

FIGURE 1-6

An example privacy policy.

- Limit the number of companies that have your personal information to those you interact with most. If you think you're unlikely to return to a site that requests registration, look somewhere else for the information you need before submitting your personal information to yet another company.

 Notes *Some people worry about little files called* **cookies** *that are placed on your computer by the servers storing the web sites you visit. In many ways, cookies are actually really useful—they store your personal preferences for a web site so that the web site is tailored to your liking when you revisit it. Cookies can't be used to retrieve personal information from your computer. They can only store information, such as information you've entered in a web page form or a record of the pages you've visited there. Your web browser also gives cookie data back only to the server that sent the cookie, not to servers of web sites you visit. However, some people consider the use of cookies a privacy violation because web site advertisers can use cookie data to gather Internet user data and build market profiles. If you're worried about this, you can set your web browser to monitor the cookies you store or you can investigate purchasing cookie protection software.*

Surfing the Internet with Children

The Internet can be an invaluable tool for young minds in several ways—a tool that many people agree should not be given up despite the potential risks involved. With a little guidance, your children can surf the Internet safely and productively, and still have fun doing so. The Internet offers many benefits for young people. Your children can access innumerable collections of research information on topics large and small. They can get help with homework by using online encyclopedias and other reference materials. The Internet can also increase their reading skills and pique their curiosity about new topics. It can improve their technology skills, which are becoming more essential as demand for these skills in the workplace grows. The Internet also allows your children to learn about other cultures and traditions and to share experiences with people from all around the world. Parents, too, can find a wealth of parenting resources online.

Here are some guidelines for making your children's Internet time as safe and productive as possible.

- Set rules for your children's online activities—when they can go online, for how long, which sites they can visit, and which sites are off limits.

- Put the computer in a room where you or another adult is often present to supervise your children's activities. Spend time with each child online, and if you're still concerned, establish a rule that they can use the Internet only with you or a trusted adult present.

- Tell your children not to give out any personal information (including personal pictures and passwords) or to use a credit card online without your permission.

- Make sure your children understand that people they meet online are not always who they say they are.

- Tell your children not to arrange to meet anyone they talk to online without your permission.

- Tell your children never to respond to messages that make them feel uncomfortable. They should ignore the sender, stop communicating with the person, and tell you or another trusted adult immediately.

- Warn your children that not all the information they find online is necessarily truthful and reliable.

- Remind your children that the rules you set for their standard communication with others apply to their Internet communication as well. Using bad or hateful language is as unacceptable on the Internet as it is everywhere else.

- Install software that monitors your children's Internet activity, prevents them from using the Internet when they aren't allowed to, and blocks content you consider inappropriate. Two popular and well-rated programs are Cyber Snoop, available at *http://www.pearlsw.com,* and Cyber Patrol, available at *http://www.learningco.com.*

 If you encounter possible criminal activity against children while online, report it at http://www.missingkids.com/cybertip/.

CHAPTER 2

Connecting to the Internet

The previous chapter described the **Internet,** explained how it works, and, with any luck, convinced you to get connected. This chapter assumes that you've decided to try it out and discusses everything you need to get on board by covering the following topics:

- The necessary equipment
- Selecting an **ISP**
- Setting up a connection
- Making the connection

The Necessary Equipment

A connection to the Internet isn't mysterious—it just requires certain hardware and software in order to work. This section describes the hardware and software necessary to set up an Internet connection.

---

 *As mentioned in the Introduction, this chapter assumes that you already have the most important piece of hardware for your Internet connection: a personal computer (PC) running either **Microsoft Windows** 95 or Windows 98. If you have a computer with Windows NT 4.0 or Windows 2000, the steps for setting up a connection outlined later in the chapter will be similar.*

---

 *New technology called **WebTV** is allowing the computer to merge with the television and vice versa. With this new technology, you don't need a computer to connect to the Internet—you can connect with your TV and accomplish most of the tasks described in this book. To connect your TV to the Internet, all you need is a regular phone line and some special hardware that plugs into your TV much like a VCR does. The hardware comes with a remote control for Internet activities. This book doesn't describe how to use WebTV, but if you're interested, you can check out a book on it.*

Hardware Choices

An Internet connection requires a physical component, called hardware. If you work at a place where a group of computers are already connected, a setup that's called a **network**, chances are your physical connection to the Internet is already established. If you want to access the Internet from home or if you want to connect a single PC at work to the Internet, you need to possess or acquire certain hardware depending on the connection type you choose. At this time, the most popular type of connection is a dial-up connection using a **modem** and a phone line.

 A modem converts signals to and from the ones and zeros (digital signals) used by your computer to the "voicelike" waveforms (analog signals) that your telephone lines can understand.

Many new computers come with modems. To determine whether you have a modem installed on your computer, follow these steps:

1 Click the Start button, and choose Settings.

2 Click Control Panel to open the Control Panel window.

3 Double-click the Modems icon.

4 See whether any modems are listed in the Modems Properties dialog box (see Figure 2-1).

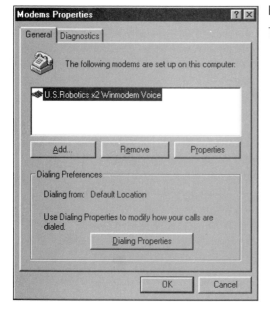

FIGURE 2-1

The Modems Properties dialog box.

5 If there are modems listed, you almost surely have a modem installed. If no modems are listed, but you think your computer has a modem, you can tell Windows to search for the modem as described in the next set of steps. Otherwise, you need to purchase and install a modem.

If you need a modem, before you make a purchase you should understand two characteristics of modems: modem speed and modem standards.

Notes *If you plan to spend a lot of time on the Internet and the speed at which you can transfer information is important to you, you might want to read on about fast-speed connections (as described in Table 2-1) before you go out and buy a modem.*

Modems are usually classified by the amount of data that they can transfer per second, which is described in kilobits per second (**Kbps**). Newer modems are usually 56.6 Kbps. The larger the Kbps number, the faster you can move around on the Internet and share information with other people. It makes sense to buy the fastest modem you can afford.

Notes *Even though modem speeds are advertised at 56.6 Kbps, your computer sends and receives other information while you are transferring the data that you want. Other people send and receive things through the Internet at the same time. In practice, this means you can transfer about a full 1.44-megabyte floppy disk's worth of information in a little over three minutes.*

Modems are also described in terms of the standards to which they conform. A 56.6-Kbps modem conforms to one of three standards: Kflex, X2, or V.90. Although the companies that make modems and the companies that connect you to the Internet are supposed to be converting to V.90, this doesn't always happen. Make sure you purchase a modem that conforms to the standard recognized by the company providing your Internet service. If you haven't yet selected a company, known as an Internet service provider, or ISP, to provide your Internet connection and you need to make a decision about a modem, you might want to jump ahead to the section "Selecting an ISP" so that the modem you buy works with your ISP account.

After you purchase a modem, you need to install it according to the manufacturer's directions. With external modems, this usually means simply turning off your computer and then plugging the modem cable into the back of your computer. If you are using an external modem, don't forget to plug it into an electrical outlet and turn it on. With internal modems, it's a little more complicated. If you have difficulty, contact your modem or computer manufacturer.

With any luck, when you turn your computer back on, Windows 95 or Windows 98 recognizes the new device and starts a **wizard** to guide you through the process of setting up the modem. If this doesn't happen, follow these steps to set up the modem:

1 Click the Start button, choose Settings, and click Control Panel.

2 Double-click the Modems icon.

3 Click Add. (If you're working from a laptop computer, your modem is probably in a small metal box about the size of a credit card. If this is your situation, you'll see the question What Type Of Modem Do You Want To Install? If you have a metal credit card–size modem, select PCMCIA Modem Card, and click Next. Follow the instructions provided.)

4 Click Next to have Windows attempt to detect the modem.

5 If Windows finds the correct modem, click Next, and then click Finish to install the modem. If the modem name Windows finds is incorrect, click Change to select the correct modem from a list. If Windows doesn't find the modem at all, click Next to display the dialog box shown in Figure 2-2.

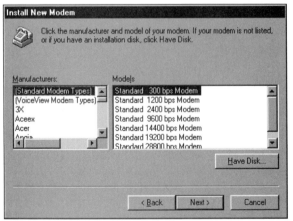

FIGURE 2-2

The Install New Modem dialog box.

6 Select the modem manufacturer and model, and click Next.

7 Select the port to which the modem is connected, and click Next to install the modem. You'll probably see a selection of COM and LPT or printer ports. Modems are generally connected to COM ports. If more than one COM port is available, consult the documentation that came with your modem for guidance.

8 Click Finish.

If you plan to spend a good deal of time on the Internet and the speed at which you can transfer information is important to you (perhaps because you're running a small business and paying employees for their time), you might not want a modem because a typical dial-up connection might not perform fast enough for you. Instead, you should consider a high-bandwidth connection. Consumer and small business high-bandwidth connections are readily available at speeds from 64 Kbps to 5 to 6 megabits per second **(Mbps)**. (One Mbps is equal to almost 1000 Kbps.) If you have several computers in an office, a single shared high-bandwidth connection can also cut costs (for instance, if you would otherwise need to add extra phone lines devoted to your dial-up connections). High-bandwidth connections require hardware different from regular dial-up modem connections, however. One reason that high-bandwidth connections are faster is that they are entirely digital; they do not have to convert the ones and zeros from your computer into the analog signals that your telephone can understand. Table 2-1 lists the most common, affordable high-bandwidth connections and the hardware requirements for each.

Notes *Not all connection types may be available in your area.*

Connection	Hardware Required
ISDN	An Integrated Services Digital Network **(ISDN)** network adapter (often incorrectly called an ISDN modem), an ISDN line set up by your phone company, and an ISP that offers ISDN connection services. Although each ISDN channel, at 64 Kbps, does not look much faster than a good modem, it's more efficient because it's all digital; it does not have to convert the ones and zeros from your computer into analog signals for your telephone. The typical ISDN connection includes two ISDN data channels.
DSL	A digital subscriber line **(DSL)** router (often incorrectly called a DSL modem) from your phone company, your phone line set up for DSL service, and a network card often provided by your phone company. DSL connections are available at speeds anywhere from hundreds of Kbps to several Mbps.
Cable	An Ethernet network adapter (also called a network interface card, or NIC) from your cable company, a cable adapter (often incorrectly called a cable modem), and a cable company that offers Internet access. Typical cable adapter connections to the Internet are also around several megabytes per second.

TABLE 2-1: High-speed connection hardware.

 *Businesses and organizations use other types of high-speed connections as well, such as **T1**, T2, T3, and T4 lines. These high-bandwidth telephone lines can handle a lot of traffic, but they are expensive to install. The monthly fee for the connection is also unaffordable for most residential and small business purposes.*

Software Choices

To browse the **World Wide Web** and make use of other Internet resources, you need Internet software. This book assumes that you'll be using **Microsoft Internet Explorer** or **Netscape Communicator** 4.51, two popular free suites of programs. Although you can use the Internet with other versions of these programs or with programs from different companies, in order to follow along with the steps in this book, you need to acquire and install either Internet Explorer 5 or Netscape Communicator 4.5 or higher. This section describes how to accomplish these tasks. Tables 2-2 and 2-3 describe the main components of Internet Explorer and Netscape Communicator and what each component program allows you to do.

Component	Use
Microsoft Internet Explorer	Browse the World Wide Web as described in Chapters 3, 4, and 5.
Microsoft Outlook Express	Send and receive **e-mail** messages as described in Chapter 6, and read and post to **newsgroups** as described in Chapter 7.
Microsoft FrontPage Express	Create your own **web page** as described in Chapter 10.
Microsoft Chat	"Converse" with people **online** as described in Chapter 8.

TABLE 2-2: Microsoft Internet Explorer components.

Component	Use
Netscape Navigator	Browse the World Wide Web as described in Chapters 3, 4, and 5.
Netscape Messenger	Send and receive e-mail messages as described in Chapter 6, and read and post to newsgroups as described in Chapter 7.
Netscape Composer	Create your own web page as described in Chapter 10.
AOL Instant Messenger	See who's online and send instant messages, as described in Chapter 8.

TABLE 2-3: Netscape Communicator 4.51 components.

If you're running Windows 98 (or a later version of Windows 95), your computer almost certainly has Internet Explorer 4 or higher already installed on it. Microsoft also bundles Internet Explorer with several of its other programs, such as the Office **suite** *of programs, so you may already have it installed and even set up from another program. To check whether you have Internet Explorer 4 or higher installed, click the Start button and choose Programs. The Internet Explorer blue lower-case "e" icon appears if you have the program installed. Alternately, you may also have a blue lowercase "e" icon next to your Start button or on your desktop.*

To see which version of Internet Explorer you're using, first open up Internet Explorer. Double-click the Internet Explorer icon (the lowercase blue "e") on your desktop. Then choose the Help menu's About Internet Explorer command. This displays the message box shown in Figure 2-3. To see which version of Netscape Communicator you're running, start **Netscape Navigator** and choose the Help menu's About Communicator command.

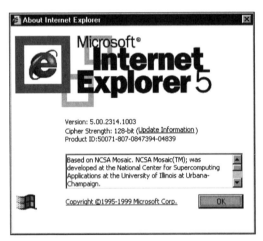

FIGURE 2-3

Checking your version of Internet Explorer.

If you already have an Internet connection and need to update your version of Internet Explorer (see Figure 2-4), enter *http:// www.microsoft.com/windows/ie/download/windows.htm* in the Address box and press Enter. When the web page appears, look at the listings for your version of Windows. Move your mouse over the Internet Explorer shown under your **operating system.** When the mouse pointer turns into a finger, click the appropriate words to select Internet Explorer 5 for your operating system, and follow the instructions onscreen to continue the **download** process.

Notes *The entire process could take several hours. If possible, it's best to do this process whenever fewer people are on the Internet. Depending on your time zone, you might want to try either early in the morning or late at night.*

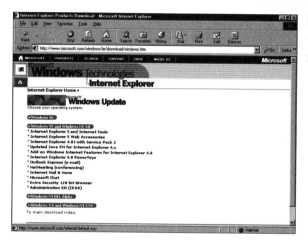

FIGURE 2-4

Downloading the latest release of Internet Explorer.

To update your version of Netscape Communicator, enter *http:// home.netscape.com/computing/download/* in the Netsite box of Navigator and click the appropriate **hyperlinks** to download what you need (see Figure 2-5).

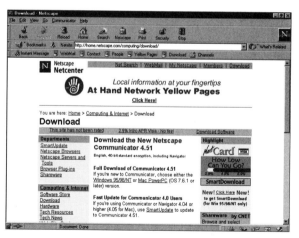

FIGURE 2-5

Downloading the latest release of Netscape Communicator.

If your computer does not have a browser installed (newer computers with Windows 95 or higher have come with a version of Internet Explorer for some time now), you can order Internet Explorer or Netscape Communicator on CD-ROM. You can order Internet Explorer for $6.95 by calling 1-800-485-2048. You can order Netscape Communicator 4.51 for $7.95 by calling 1-800-591-4805. In either case, have your billing and shipping names and addresses and your credit card number handy and be prepared to tell the sales representative which **operating system** you use (Windows 95 or Windows 98).

Selecting an ISP

Using the Internet is free, but for most people, connecting to it isn't. Companies called Internet service providers (ISPs) let you access the Internet for a monthly fee. If you think of the Internet as an Information Superhighway, an ISP charges entrance fees at the on-ramps. Once you get on, however, you're free to go anywhere—regardless of whether your destination is St. Petersburg, Florida, or St. Petersburg, Russia. Only a few destinations charge visiting fees. Before you choose an ISP, you have four main factors to consider: service, cost, support for connection type, and features offered.

If you already have an Internet connection and are looking to find a new, better one, search The List at http://thelist.internet.com/ *for ISPs in your area. To see how national ISPs and **online services** compare, check out ZDNet's ISP shopping guides at* http://www.zdnet.com/products/internetuser/isp.html.

*Some ISPs are called online services because they provide and organize Internet content in addition to providing Internet access. For example, they may host newsgroups browsable only by their members, they may provide their own software or Internet tools, and they may have **web sites** with customizable pages for their customers' convenience.*

First and foremost, it's important that the ISP you choose provides good service. This means that the provider's computers run smoothly so you can dependably make your connection. It also means that you can reach your ISP's technical support technicians when you need help. To find an ISP that provides good service, ask your friends, coworkers, and acquaintances about the companies they use and whether they have been pleased with their service. Then make a few phone calls to ask the companies about their support, and try out one or more yourself. Ideally, look for an ISP with 24-hour, seven-day-a-week free telephone support that's friendly and easy to use. If an ISP's only means of providing support is through a web page or via e-mail, it's not much help to you if you have problems connecting.

 Many providers offer a free trial period for the first month of service. If you want to try out an ISP, make use of the trial period to test the connection at various times during the day to determine whether high traffic slows down the service or prevents you from connecting.

Second, determine the costs of making your connection. Confirm that the connection requires a local or toll-free call. If you will be connecting outside of the United States or Canada, make sure that your access number keeps your toll charges to a minimum. To compare total costs of one plan with another, inquire about any one-time startup charges and then estimate the amount of time you think you'll spend online. Most ISPs offer inexpensive plans (for under $10 a month), but these plans usually include only a few hours of connection time. If you expect to use the Internet only to send the occasional e-mail message, a plan like this might work well for you. However, if you anticipate that you, your coworkers, or your family members will spend a lot of time connected to the Internet, you should probably opt for an unlimited-usage plan.

Third, make sure you find an ISP that supports the type of connection you intend to make. For instance, if you have a fast, 56-Kbps modem, you won't be able to exploit its potential if your ISP doesn't offer connections at that speed. You also need to make sure that your ISP recognizes the standard your modem uses. If you're considering a high-bandwidth connection (either now or in the foreseeable future), you need an ISP that offers accounts for that connection type. Table 2-4 describes some high-speed connections and the benefits of each.

 The "Hardware Choices" section and Table 2-1 earlier in this chapter describe the hardware that's necessary for the high-bandwidth connections explained in this book.

Connection	Description
Cable modem	A small but growing percentage of homes with cable TV have the option of adding cable Internet access. If cable Internet access is available in your community, it's definitely worth considering, especially because it's easy to set up (your cable company does most of the work for you) and is competitively priced. A possible drawback of cable connections is that you share bandwidth with other cable Internet users in your community. As long as only a few people jump on the bandwagon with you, you'll have the bandwidth practically to yourself. But if cable Internet connections become popular in your community, your speed may be far from the megabits per second that the cable salesperson perhaps led you to expect.
ISDN	ISDN service is readily available in many communities, and it's becoming easier to install. It's also attractively priced and has a history of reliability. Basic ISDN service is available at 128 Kbps. Enhanced ISDN services are available in 64 Kbps increments up to several Mbps.
DSL	Unlike ISDN and regular dial-up connections, a DSL connection is permanent (always on). It offers speeds of 144 Kbps to around 8 Mbps for viewing information on the Internet. (It's usually priced on a scale with the speed of connection.)

TABLE 2-4: Three popular high-speed connection options.

Last, if you want to establish your own presence on the World Wide Web (described in Chapter 10), make sure that your account includes **server** space for web page hosting. Many ISPs include a few megabytes of space for a web page, which is all that's necessary for most personal web pages. Find out whether web space is available with your ISP (perhaps at an additional cost).

Setting Up a Connection

If your ISP provides you with software, you can use this software to quickly and easily set up your Internet connection. If, however, you don't have any software for your ISP, you can use features provided by your **web browser** to set up your Internet connection. This section describes how.

Using Internet Explorer's Internet Connection Wizard

If you're using Internet Explorer, you can use the **Internet Connection Wizard** that comes with the program to set up an Internet connection. If you're connecting to the Internet through an ISP, make sure you know the phone number, user name, and **password** that you want to use to connect to that ISP. You'll also need the names of your ISP's mail servers. They should look something like **pop**.yourisp.com and **smtp**.yourisp.com. If this is the first time you're connecting to an ISP, ask the ISP for that information first. Once you have all of this information, you're ready to use the Internet Connection Wizard. To do so, follow these steps:

 If you're using Netscape Communicator, skip to the next section, "Setting Up Netscape Communicator."

---

1 Click the Start button.

2 Choose Programs, choose Accessories, choose Communications (if available), and then click Internet Connection Wizard to start the wizard.

 If you have a Connect To The Internet icon on your Windows desktop, you can also double-click this icon to start the Internet Connection Wizard.

---

3 If you've never used the Internet Connection Wizard before, Windows might display an introductory dialog box. Click Next.

4 In the dialog box shown in Figure 2-6, click an option button to tell the Internet Connection Wizard how you want to set up your Internet account. (Step 5 continues on the assumption that you clicked the third option button.)

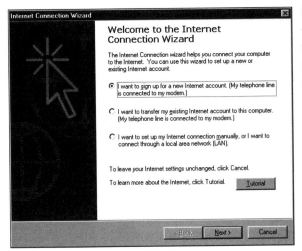

FIGURE 2-6

The Internet Connection Wizard helps you set up and describe an Internet connection.

If you click the first option button, you can select and configure a new account listed on the Microsoft Referral Service. If you don't know which ISP you want to use and would like to try one out, this is the easiest way to do so because the Internet Connection Wizard does most of the setup work for you. The Internet Connection Wizard makes a toll-free call and displays a list of ISPs in your area, as shown in Figure 2-7. Select an ISP from the list, click Next, and follow the instructions onscreen for setting up the ISP you selected.

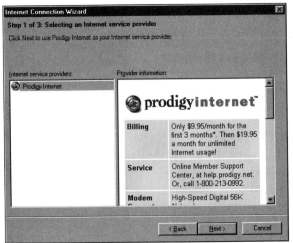

FIGURE 2-7

Selecting an ISP from the Microsoft Referral Service.

If you already have an account configured on another computer and want to see whether the Internet Connection Wizard can configure it automatically, click the second option button. The Internet Connection Wizard makes a toll-free call and displays a list of ISPs that support the automatic configuration feature. If your ISP is listed, select it and click Next. The Internet Connection Wizard connects to your ISP and begins the process of automatically configuring your account. Your ISP probably requests your user name and password and other information as required.

5 After you click the third option button, click the appropriate option button in the next dialog box to tell Internet Explorer whether you're creating a dial-up connection (I Connect Through A Phone Line Or Modem) or an Internet connection over a network (I Connect Through A Local Area Network). If you're creating an Internet connection over a network, ask the network administrator for help regarding the network setup and skip to step 10.

6 Select your modem, and click Next.

7 Enter the phone number your ISP gave you to connect, and click Next.

8 Enter your user name and password for making the connection, and click Next.

9 Name the connection, and click Next. This is important if you have more than one account. For example, you might have one account named "Work" and another named "Personal."

10 Click the Yes option button, and click Next to set up an e-mail account with your ISP.

11 Click the Create A New Internet Mail Account option button, and click Next to set up a new account.

12 In the text box provided, enter your name as you would like people to see it when they receive messages from you and click Next.

13 In the text box provided, enter your e-mail address as provided by your ISP, and click Next.

14 Enter the addresses of your incoming and outgoing mail servers as provided by your ISP (see Figure 2-8), and click Next.

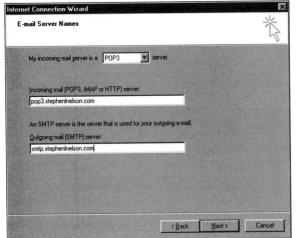

FIGURE 2-8

Entering information required to send and receive Internet mail.

15 Enter your e-mail account name and password. If you don't have to worry about anyone else using your computer for e-mail, select the Remember Password check box. In this way, **Microsoft Outlook Express** won't prompt you for your password to send or receive e-mail. This feature is helpful if you tend to forget passwords, but it means that anyone using your computer can receive your new messages and read them.

16 Select the Log On Using Secure Password Authentication check box if your ISP requires you to do so. If you're not sure, ask your ISP.

17 Click Next, select the last check box to test your connection immediately, and click Finish. Your computer will test your connection to your ISP.

Setting Up Netscape Communicator

The first time you start Netscape Communicator, it prompts you to create a new profile, which will contain your settings. To set up Netscape Communicator, follow these steps:

1 Click Next to begin.

2 Enter your name and complete e-mail address as shown in Figure 2-9, and click Next.

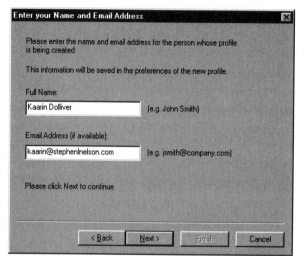

FIGURE 2-9

Setting up an e-mail account.

3 Name your profile and accept the default profile storage location by clicking Next.

4 Enter the address of your outgoing e-mail server as given to you by your ISP, and click Next.

5 In the dialog box shown in Figure 2-10, enter the user name your ISP gave you for retrieving your e-mail, enter your incoming e-mail server's address, select the mail server type, and click Next. If you have any questions about what to enter, contact your ISP.

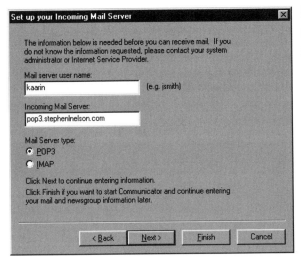

FIGURE 2-10

Setting up the incoming mail server.

6 Enter the address of your newsgroup server. Select the Secure check box if your ISP specified that you should do so. The default port address is usually correct, but if you can't get newsgroups to work, you may need to contact your ISP for the port address.

7 Click Finish to begin using your profile.

 If you make a mistake while setting up your profile, you can change your settings by choosing the Edit menu's Preferences command in Netscape Navigator.

If you're making a **dial-up networking** connection and haven't used the Internet Connection Wizard before to set up the connection, you must do so manually. Follow these steps:

1 Click the Start button, choose Programs, choose Accessories, choose Communications (if available), and click Dial-Up Networking to display the Dial-Up Networking window shown in Figure 2-11.

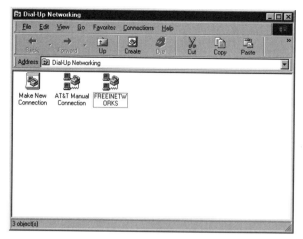

FIGURE 2-11

The Dial-Up Networking window.

2 Double-click the Make New Connection icon to display the dialog box shown in Figure 2-12.

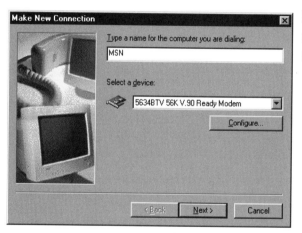

FIGURE 2-12

Setting up a new connection.

3 Enter a name describing the connection. If you have more than one ISP, you might want to name the connection after the ISP. If you have multiple connections for different people using the computer, you might want to name the connection after the person who will use it.

4 Select the modem you'll use for the connection, and click Next.

5 Enter the access phone number for your ISP, and click Next.

6 Click Finish.

Making the Connection

The rest of the chapters in this book describe what you can do online once you're connected, so before you can follow a set of steps to accomplish a task, you must first make your **Internet connection.** If you're connected over a network or using a high-speed connection, as soon as you open your web browser or click a button to access Internet information, the connection may be made automatically for you. Depending on your Internet service provider, if you're making a dial-up networking connection and request information from the Internet, you might be prompted to make the dial-up networking connection. If this isn't the case, you can easily connect manually.

To manually initiate a dial-up connection, follow these steps:

1 Click the Start button, choose Programs, choose Accessories, choose Communications (if available), and click Dial-Up Networking to display the Dial-Up Networking window.

2 Double-click the icon for the connection you want to make to display the Connect To dialog box shown in Figure 2-13.

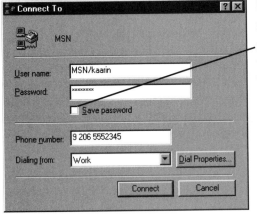

FIGURE 2-13

Connecting to your ISP.

Select the Save Password check box to have your computer remember your password so you don't have to enter it each time you connect.

3 Verify your user name, enter your **password** if necessary, and verify your dialing location and the phone number to be dialed.

4 Click Connect. You'll probably hear a dial tone and then dialing. Then your modem will probably make some screeching sounds for a few seconds.

If you don't hear any sounds coming from your modem when you attempt to connect, verify that the phone line is firmly connected to the back of the modem and into the wall jack. If your modem has two slots for a phone cord, see whether you can find labels on the slots. If you can find a label marked "line," use this slot for plugging the modem into the wall. If the slots aren't labeled, just give each one a try. If you have an external modem, verify that the modem is plugged in and turned on and that the cables are firmly connected to the back of the modem and to the computer. If you still don't get a dial tone, verify that the phone line and phone cord work. Plug a regular telephone into the end of the phone line and see whether you hear a dial tone and can dial out. If you can't, contact your telephone company to repair the line.

If your modem continues to make all sorts of noise for an extended period of time and doesn't eventually connect, cancel the connection and try again. This happens frequently with modems and does not signal a problem.

If your modem dials but can't establish a connection, the server you are dialing might be out of service. Try dialing a backup number, or wait a few minutes and dial again. Some ISPs might let you choose from a long list of numbers to dial. If the ones in your area don't work, try dialing a number in a different location.

To manually disconnect, double-click the little green boxes in the lower right corner of the Windows taskbar (next to the clock) and click Disconnect in the message box.

If your modem establishes a connection but then disconnects, make sure that you entered your user name and password correctly. Click the Start button, choose Programs, choose Accessories, choose Communications (if you have this option), and click Dial-Up Networking. Double-click the icon for the connection you're trying to make to display the Connect To dialog box. Make sure your user name, password, and the telephone number you're trying to dial are correct.

CHAPTER 3

World Wide Web Basics

One of the hottest areas of the **Internet** is the World Wide Web. The **World Wide Web** lets you view special files, called **web pages.** These pages are usually connected to one another with highlighted pictures or underlined text known as **hyperlinks.** You can click on these hyperlinks to "navigate" from web page to web page. The Web is very easy to use—much easier than **e-mail**, for example. This chapter goes over the following important Web-related concepts and activities:

- Defining some important terms
- Simple navigation techniques
- Working with **Internet Explorer**
- Working with **Netscape Navigator**

Defining Some Important Terms

As noted previously, the Web consists of web pages connected by hyperlinks. To understand this definition, you need to know the meaning of two key terms, *web page* and *hyperlink*.

A *web page* is a file that typically uses multiple media for communicating information. For example, text is one medium. Pictures are another. Sound is still another. So web pages are files that use text, pictures, and sometimes even sound or video. Figure 3-1 shows an ESPN web page. Note that it uses multiple media—both text and pictures.

FIGURE 3-1

The main web page of the ESPN web site.

The web page address appears here.

Web pages are the building blocks of the Web. A group of web pages linked together and stored in the same place make up a **web site**. For example, the ESPN web site is made up of several web pages. Some pages are devoted to a single sport, others contain TV listings, and others contain news highlights or products you can buy.

The unique feature of web pages is that they also include hyperlinks. A *hyperlink,* essentially, is an address that points to another Internet resource, such as a web page. When you click a hyperlink, you're actually telling your browser to retrieve and then display the resource identified by the hyperlink. In Figure 3-1, for example, there are several hyperlinks. The promotional squares beside the title banner are hyperlinks. All the underlined segments of text are hyperlinks as well. If you click the Soccer hyperlink from the list on the left, your **web browser** retrieves a web page with the latest soccer news and links to national and international soccer league information (see Figure 3-2).

FIGURE 3-2

A web page such as this appears after you click the Soccer hyperlink.

You now know how to view web pages and work with hyperlinks. But you should also learn how web page addresses work so you can use them as you browse web pages. A web page address is also known by the term *uniform resource locator,* or **URL.**

A URL is made up of four parts:

- A code that identifies the address as a World Wide Web page
- The name of the computer, called a web **server,** that stores the web page
- The folder location of the web page
- The web page name

If you look at Figure 3-2, you'll notice that its address is

http://espn.go.com/soccer/index.html

The *http://* part of this address is the code that identifies the address as a World Wide Web page. (Despite what you may have heard, the *www* that often follows the double slashes is not absolutely required for all web page addresses.) The *espn.go.com* part of the address is the name of the ESPN web server. The */soccer/* part of the address is the folder holding the web page. Finally, *index.html* is the actual web page name.

Simple Navigation Techniques

To view a web page, start your web browser. If you aren't connected to the Internet, **Microsoft Windows** or your web browser might prompt you for the information needed to make this connection. You might, for example, need to supply a password. In any event, your web browser soon begins loading a **home page** such as the one shown in Figure 3-3, which is simply a default web page.

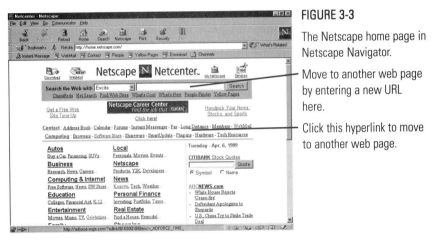

FIGURE 3-3

The Netscape home page in Netscape Navigator.

Move to another web page by entering a new URL here.

Click this hyperlink to move to another web page.

 If you attempt to display a web page and your web browser returns a message saying that the page cannot be displayed or could not be found, you can remedy this common problem in a couple of ways. First, verify that the URL is correctly spelled and punctuated. If it is, and you're attempting to access a specific page in a specific folder on a web site, try going to the web site's home page and clicking hyperlinks to access the page you want. The web site publisher may have changed the folder or filename you're looking for. Second, if all else fails, try again at a later time. The web server might be busy or out of service, or your Internet connection might be down.

Clicking Hyperlinks

To move to another page, click a hyperlink. As previously mentioned, hyperlinks often appear as underlined text. They also appear as clickable buttons. You can always tell whether a section of text is a hyperlink, however, by moving the mouse pointer over it. When you do so, the mouse pointer changes to a pointing finger.

Entering URLs

You can also move to another web page by typing the web page's address, or URL, in the Address or Location box. (The box that you choose depends on whether you are using Microsoft Internet Explorer or **Netscape Communicator** and the version of the browser that you currently have installed.) You can return to your home page at any time by clicking the Home toolbar button.

 When entering URLs, you don't need to enter the entire address. Web page addresses almost always begin with http://, so you can leave this part out. You can also leave out the last slash (/) of the address, if the address ends with one. And if you've visited the web page in the past few days, your web browser may recognize the address as you type it. If you're using Internet Explorer, use the arrow keys to select the URL you want to return to from the drop-down list box. If you're using Netscape Navigator, press the Enter key to go to the address Netscape completes for you.

If you don't know the address for a site you want to visit on the World Wide Web, you can often successfully guess it. Here's how:

- Many URLs begin with the letters *www*. Enter this first, followed by a period.

- Enter the name of the business, organization, or institution next, followed by a period. Don't include spaces. If the name is very long, it's probably abbreviated. Think of any likely abbreviations.

- For U.S. web pages, enter the domain *.com* for a commercial organization, *.gov* for a governmental organization, *.edu* for an educational institution, *.org* for a nonprofit organization, or *.mil* for a military organization. Or if the page you want to display is international, enter the country's two-letter domain code. The official list of country codes is located at *www.iana.org/cctld.html*.

It might take a few attempts, but with a little trial and error, an educated guess often works.

Here are a couple of examples. Suppose you want to see the home page for the U.S. Postal Service. You might try the following URLs:

www.ps.gov

www.postalservice.gov

www.usps.gov

If one doesn't work, your web browser either displays an incorrect page or beeps at you. You can then try the next URL. In this case, the third time's the charm.

Here's another example. Suppose you want to visit the home page for Odense University in Denmark. You might try the following URL:

www.ou.dk

And you'd be right!

Moving Back and Forth

You can move between web pages in a web browser by clicking the toolbar buttons labeled Back and Forward (see Figure 3-4). You can move to a web page you've previously viewed by clicking the Back toolbar button. After you click the Back toolbar button, you can move to the page you viewed before clicking Back by clicking the Forward toolbar button.

FIGURE 3-4

The Back and Forward toolbar buttons in Internet Explorer and Netscape Navigator.

Stopping and Requesting an Updated Copy of a Web Page

To tell your web browser to stop loading a web page, click the Stop toolbar button (see Figure 3-5). You might want to stop loading a web page if retrieving the page is taking a long time—too long for you to wait.

FIGURE 3-5

The Stop, Refresh, and Reload toolbar buttons.

To **download** an updated copy of a web page, click the Refresh toolbar button if you're using Internet Explorer or click the Reload toolbar button if you're using Netscape Navigator (see Figure 3-5). You might want to do this if you're viewing a web page with information that changes frequently, such as the price of a stock, or if you had to click the Stop toolbar button because a web page was taking too long to appear.

Working with Internet Explorer

This next section describes how to work with some of the special features of Internet Explorer. If you're using Netscape Navigator, you might want to skip ahead to the section "Working with Netscape Navigator" to learn about the features unique to that program.

Designating a Home Page

If you don't like the web page that appears each time you start Internet Explorer, you can tell Internet Explorer to display a different page (called a start page or a home page) at startup.

 Notes The term home page *has two separate meanings. First,* home page *can describe the web page that initially appears when you start your web browser. Second, the term* home page *can describe the main web page of any web site. So your home page would be a web page you've created and published on the web, either singly or as the main web page of a multipage web site. This section of the chapter uses the first definition.*

To change your home page, follow these steps:

1 Choose the Tools menu's Internet Options command to display the dialog box shown in Figure 3-6.

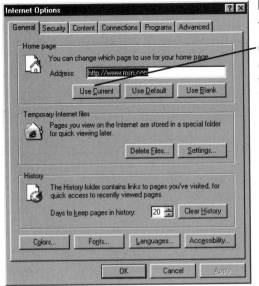

FIGURE 3-6

The Internet Options dialog box.

Click Use Current instead of entering a URL to use the page you're currently viewing as your home page.

2   In the Home Page section, enter a web page address in the Address box. Alternately, if you want to use the current web page in your browser, you can make that your home page by clicking Use Current.

3   Click OK.

 To display your home page, click the Home toolbar button. It's usually best to pick for your home page a web page that you most frequently visit or that you can easily use as a springboard to browse the World Wide Web. Many web sites allow you to customize your home page by choosing which information and hyperlinks you want included on the page.

Keeping a List of Favorite Web Pages

You can add a web page address to a special folder of favorite web pages, called the **Favorites** folder. By designating a web page as a favorite, you can easily access it in the future without needing to type its URL. This is especially useful for web pages you visit frequently or that have long URLs.

To make a web page a favorite, first open the web page. Then choose the Favorites menu's Add To Favorites command, and click OK in the Add Favorite dialog box (see Figure 3-7). To view the web page later, choose the web page from the Favorites bar or the Favorites menu.

FIGURE 3-7

The Add Favorite dialog box.

 To display the Favorites bar, click the Favorites toolbar button. To hide the Favorites bar, click its Close button or click the Favorites toolbar button again.

Finding Pages Related to the One Displayed

If you find a web page that you like very much and would like to browse others that might have similar content, choose the Tools menu's Show Related Links command. This opens the Search bar and displays a list of hyperlinks to related web pages, as shown in Figure 3-8.

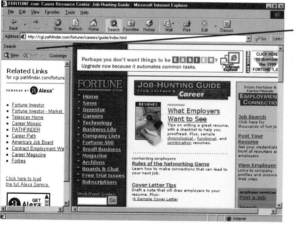

FIGURE 3-8

The Search bar showing a list of hyperlinks to related web pages.

Viewing a History Log of Web Pages You've Visited

Clicking the History toolbar button opens a new pane in Internet Explorer that lists the web sites you've visited in the past 20 days (see Figure 3-9).

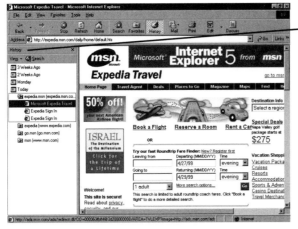

FIGURE 3-9

The History bar shows a record of the web pages you've recently viewed.

To see the web sites you visited during a particular week or day, click the week or day in the History bar. To return to one of the web sites, click its entry in the list.

 To close the History bar, click its Close button or click the History toolbar button again.

If you want to cover your web-browsing tracks, clear your history log by following these steps:

1 Choose the Tools menu's Internet Options command to display the dialog box shown in Figure 3-10.

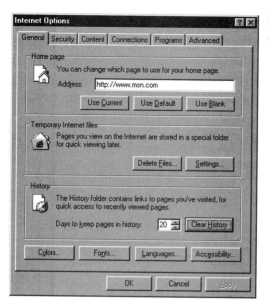

FIGURE 3-10

The Internet Options dialog box.

2 Click Clear History.

3 When Internet Explorer requests confirmation (Delete All Items In Your History Folder?), click Yes.

 To delete a single web page listed in the History bar, right-click it and then choose the shortcut menu's Delete command.

Downloading Files

Many hyperlinks on the Internet point to downloadable files. Downloading a file means copying the file from the Internet to your computer. It's possible to download many types of files from the Internet. Typically, the programs that people download from the Internet fall into two categories: programs available for use without charge or limitation are known as "freeware"; programs that come with a free evaluation period are known as "**shareware.**" Shareware programs are usually set up to stop working after the evaluation period expires. People also download documents, updated drivers for hardware, and all sorts of information. When you click a hyperlink that points to a downloadable file, Internet Explorer displays the dialog box shown in Figure 3-11.

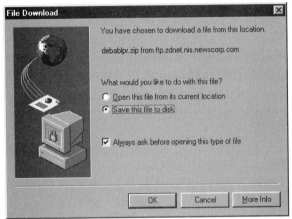

FIGURE 3-11

The File Download dialog box.

To download the file, click the Save This Program To Disk option button and click OK. Use the Save As dialog box to specify a filename and a location for saving the file, and click Save. When you click Save, the download process begins and Internet Explorer displays a progress bar so that you can monitor the progress of the download.

 Be prudent about the files you download because you can easily get ***viruses*** *from downloaded files. Download files only from sources you trust. If you frequently download files from the Internet, it's a good idea to get virus-protection software. Popular sources include Norton AntiVirus, which is available at* http://www.symantec.com/nav/index.html, *and Norman Virus Control, which is available at* http://www.norman.com/local/.

 It's a good practice to pay attention to the size and number of the files you download. Depending on the speed of your Internet connection, large files (such as programs) may take a long time to download. Depending on the size of your hard drive, downloaded files may also quickly fill up your free disk space.

Finding Text in a Web Page

If the page you're viewing is large and contains a lot of text, you might have difficulty finding the information you're looking for. To remedy this, use Internet Explorer's Find feature. To do so, follow these steps:

1 Choose the Edit menu's Find (On This Page) command to display the dialog box shown in Figure 3-12.

FIGURE 3-12

The Find dialog box.

2 Enter the text you're searching for in the Find What box.

3 Select the Match Whole Word Only check box to have Internet Explorer skip occurrences of letters that make up part of a larger word.

4 Select the Match Case check box to search on the case (upper or lower) you entered.

5 Use the Direction option buttons to specify where you want to begin the search.

6 Click Find Next.

 You can start the Find feature in Internet Explorer by pressing Ctrl+F.

Printing and Saving Web Pages

You can print a web page. You can also save the web pages you view. To print a web page, click the Print toolbar button. To specify print options, choose the File menu's Print command and use the Print dialog box to describe how you want the web page printed.

To save a web page, choose the File menu's Save As command. Use the Save Web Page dialog box (see Figure 3-13) to name the web page file and specify the file type and location where you want the file saved.

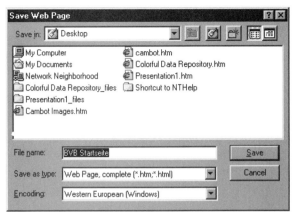

FIGURE 3-13

The Save Web Page dialog box.

To save all the files (such as graphic and sound files) that make up the web page separately in their original formats, select Web Page, Complete from the Save As Type drop-down list box. To save all the files that make up the web page in a single file, select Web Archive. To save all the formatting and layout information on the web page without the graphics or sound, select Web Page, **HTML** only. To save only the text, choose Text Only.

 To save only a picture on a web page, right-click the picture and choose the shortcut menu's Save Picture As command. Or choose Set As Wallpaper to use the picture as a wallpaper for your Windows desktop.

Listening to Internet Radio

Internet Explorer has a great new feature you can use to listen to the radio at your computer. To begin, choose the View menu's Toolbars command and then choose Radio from the submenu. This displays the Radio toolbar. Click the Radio Stations toolbar button, and choose Radio Station Guide from the menu to display a web page similar to that shown in Figure 3-14.

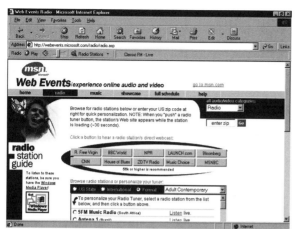

FIGURE 3-14

The Web Events Radio web page.

Click either the U.S. State, Country, or Format option button, and use the drop-down list box to select the state, country, or music format you want to use to browse. When you find a station you want to try, click the Listen hyperlink. If you like the station and think you'll want to listen to it again, you can "program" the Web Events Radio web page much as you would program an automobile radio. Just click the option button next to the station you like, and then click one of the gray buttons above the list of stations to assign that button to the station you chose.

Customizing Internet Explorer

You can customize Internet Explorer in several ways. To access most of Internet Explorer's customization options, choose the Tools menu's Internet Options command to display the Internet Options dialog box (refer to Figure 3-10).

On the General tab, click Delete Files if you need to free up space on your hard disk. This dumps the local copies of files you've recently viewed, known as your Internet cache.

Click the Security tab to set the security levels for various web site categories (called zones). Click an icon at the top to select a zone, and then use the slider to set the security for the zone you selected. With a higher security setting, Internet Explorer displays more warnings before you download potentially offensive material. If you choose the Local **Intranet**, Trusted Sites, or Restricted Sites zone, you can click Sites to add web sites to the zone you selected.

Click the Content tab to enable the Content Advisor feature. The Content Advisor allows you to restrict sites based on Language, Nudity, Sex, and Violence ratings levels.

 Chapter 1 describes how to set security options in Internet Explorer. It also describes how you can use third-party software to restrict the content that you (or your children) can view in your browser.

If you have a slow connection, click the Advanced tab and clear the Play Videos and Play Sounds check boxes to prevent Internet Explorer from downloading sounds or videos, as shown in Figure 3-15.

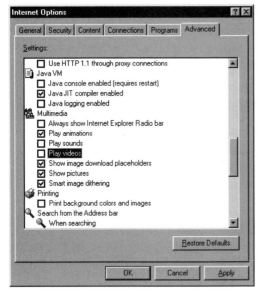

FIGURE 3-15

The Advanced tab of the Internet Options dialog box.

Working with Netscape Navigator

This section describes how to work with some of the special features of Netscape Navigator. If you've read the previous section or have ever worked with Internet Explorer before, you'll find that Netscape Navigator works in much the same way.

Designating a Home Page

If you don't like the web page that appears each time you start Netscape Navigator, you can tell it to display a different page (called a start page or a home page) at startup. To change your home page, follow these steps:

1   Choose the Edit menu's Preferences command to display the dialog box shown in Figure 3-16.

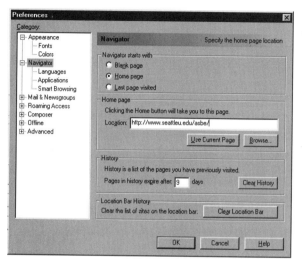

FIGURE 3-16

The Preferences dialog box.

2   Select Navigator from the Category list, and enter a web page address in the Location box.

3   Click OK.

 To display your home page, click the Home toolbar button. You probably want to pick a web page other than the default Netscape home page because you can use the My Netscape toolbar button to quickly access your personal Netscape home page.

Bookmarking Web Pages You Want to Revisit

You can **bookmark** a web page so that you can easily access it in the future without needing to type its URL. This is especially useful for those web pages you frequently visit or that have long URLs.

To bookmark a web page, first open the web page. Then click the Bookmarks toolbar button, and choose Add Bookmark. To visit a bookmarked web page, click the Bookmarks toolbar button, and choose the web page from the drop-down menu. To edit your list of Bookmarks, click the Bookmarks toolbar button and choose Edit Bookmarks to display a window similar to that shown in Figure 3-17.

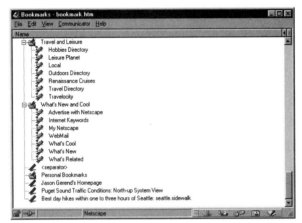

FIGURE 3-17

The Bookmarks window.

To delete a Bookmark, right-click it in the list and choose Delete Bookmark from the shortcut menu. To rename a Bookmark, right-click it in the list and choose Bookmark Properties from the shortcut menu. Then enter a new name in the Name box.

Finding Pages Related to the One Displayed

If you find a web page that appeals to you, and you would like to visit others that might have similar content, click the What's Related toolbar button next to the Location bar. This opens a drop-down menu of related web pages similar to that shown in Figure 3-18. Choose a page from the menu to go to that page.

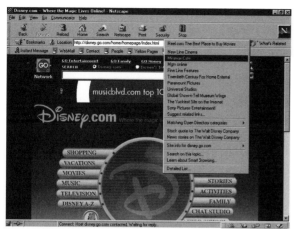

FIGURE 3-18

A list of related web pages.

Returning to Previously Viewed Web Pages

You can see a complete list of URLs you've visited along with information such as when you last visited them and how many times you've visited them. Choose the Communicator menu's Tools command and then choose the History command from the submenu to display a History window similar to that shown in Figure 3-19.

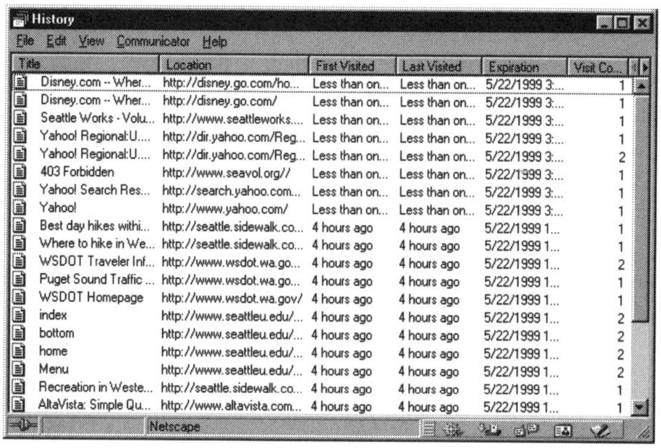

FIGURE 3-19

The History window.

Use the View menu commands to sort your history list for easy navigation. To return to a web page listed in the History window, double-click that page in the list. To delete a URL from your history list, right-click the page and choose the shortcut menu's Delete command. To clear your history list, follow these steps:

1   Choose the Edit menu's Preferences command in either the Netscape program window or in the History window.

2   Select Navigator from the Categories list, and click Clear History.

Downloading Files

Many hyperlinks on the Internet point to downloadable files. Downloading a file means copying the file from the Internet to your computer. It's possible to download many types of files from the Internet. People typically download programs from the Internet that fall into two categories: programs available for use without charge or limitation are known as "freeware"; programs that come with a free evaluation period are known as "**shareware**." Shareware programs are usually set up to stop working after the evaluation period expires. People also download documents, updated drivers for hardware, and all sorts of information. When you click a hyperlink that points to a downloadable file, Netscape Navigator displays the dialog box shown in Figure 3-20.

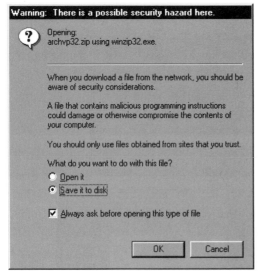

FIGURE 3-20

The Warning dialog box.

To download a file, click the Save It To Disk option button and click OK. Use the Save As dialog box to specify a filename and a location for saving the file, and click Save. When you click Save, the download process begins and Netscape Navigator displays a progress bar so that you can monitor the progress of the download.

*An easy way to get computer **viruses** is by downloading files from unknown sources. Download files only from sources you trust.*

 Be aware of the size and number of the files you download as well. Depending on the speed of your Internet connection, large files (such as programs) may take a long time to download. Depending on the size of your hard drive, downloaded files may also quickly fill up your free disk space.

Finding Text in a Web Page

To help you find the information you're looking for on a web page that contains a lot of text, use Netscape's Find feature. To do so, follow these steps:

1 Choose the Edit menu's Find In Page command to display the dialog box shown in Figure 3-21.

FIGURE 3-21

The Find dialog box.

2 Enter the text you're searching for in the Find What box.

3 Select the Match Case check box if you want Netscape Navigator to pay attention to the letter case you used.

4 Use the Direction option buttons to specify where you want Netscape Navigator to begin the search.

5 Click Find Next.

 You can start the Find feature in Netscape Navigator by pressing Ctrl+F.

Printing and Saving Web Pages

You can print and save the web pages you view. To print a web page, click the Print toolbar button and then click OK in the Print dialog box.

To save a web page, choose the File menu's Save As command. Use the dialog box shown in Figure 3-22 to name the web page file and specify where you want the file saved.

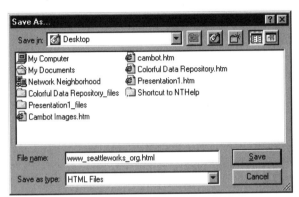

FIGURE 3-22

The Save As dialog box.

CHAPTER 4

Finding Information

The **Internet** and especially the **World Wide Web** are treasure troves of information, but sifting through all that material to find what you want can be a challenge—and sometimes a daunting one. Fortunately, the Internet itself provides powerful **search engines** that you can use to locate information. This chapter explains how you use these tools by discussing the following topics:

- Understanding how search engines work
- Using a directory search engine
- Using an index search engine
- Popular search engines

Understanding How Search Engines Work

Search engines work in two basic ways: as directories and as indexes. You're probably familiar with how both directories and indexes work, but just to make sure, let's review them.

 Notes You don't pay anything to use a search engine. Search engines make their money by selling advertising.

A directory search engine works very much like the business telephone directory that your local phone company supplies. Usually referred to as the Yellow Pages, this phone book organizes businesses by category and subcategory, with the entries in a category appearing in alphabetical order. To use the phone book directory, you first find a category (perhaps "Automobiles") and then a subcategory ("Automobiles—Repair"). After you've done this, you search through the entries of the subcategory until you find the one you want.

Many Internet search engines work in a similar fashion. You find the information you're looking for—in the form of a **web page** or a set of web pages—by searching through categories and subcategories of information.

An index search engine works like the index in the back of a book such as this Smart Guide provides. To use an index, you look up a term or phrase in an index of terms and phrases. Following the entry, the index lists the pages where the term or phrase you specified is used.

Index search engines work in the same basic way. You type a term or phrase in a text box and then click a button that's labeled something like "Search" or "Find" or "Look Up." The index search engine then looks up the term or phrase in its index. If the search is successful—and it almost always is—you get a list of web pages that use the term or phrase.

 Spider *is the technical term for the software that actually does the searching for the search engines.*

This chapter describes how to use both types of search engines. Before you move on, however, here are three more points to note about search engines: First, most search engines that you've heard of or that you'll encounter aren't "purebreds" anymore. You probably won't find a search engine that's solely a directory; you also won't encounter a search engine that's solely an index. All the popular search engines are essentially hybrids now and work both as directory and index search engines. (However, each type of search engine has its strengths and weaknesses.)

Second, because the information on the Internet and the World Wide Web is constantly changing, all search engines are out of date to varying degrees. Even if some visible bit of new information appears on the Web—say, on a prominent **web site**—it takes at least several days and often several weeks before the large search engines find the new information and then update their directories or indexes.

Third, you'll find it helpful to learn how to use more than one search engine. Sometimes a search engine is slow or unavailable, so it's efficient to have a backup. Sometimes one search engine finds something that another search engine misses, so it's good to know more than one way to track down information.

*Once you find a search engine you want to use, add it to your list of favorites (if you're working with **Microsoft Internet Explorer**) or your list of **bookmarks** (if you're working with **Netscape Navigator**). The steps for adding favorites and bookmarks are described in Chapter 3.*

Using a Directory Search Engine

As mentioned previously, a directory search engine works like a business telephone directory. To demonstrate how this works, suppose you want to look for information about traveling to Florida using the Yahoo! search engine. To do this, follow these steps:

1   Enter the **URL** for the Yahoo! search engine, *www.yahoo.com*, in the Address box provided by the **web browser.** Your web browser retrieves the Yahoo! **home page** (see Figure 4-1).

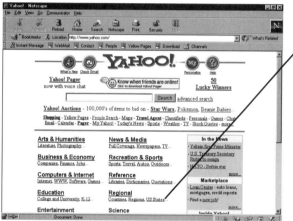

FIGURE 4-1

The Yahoo! home page.

The U.S. States hyperlink.

The interfaces for the search engines described here change frequently, so the search engine you see might look a little different from the one shown and described in this chapter. Although it might look different, the way in which the search engine works is likely to be the same.

2   Click the category that most closely matches the information you want to find. For example, to search for information about traveling to Florida, you could start by clicking the U.S. States **hyperlink**. Yahoo! then returns a web page listing the states (see Figure 4-2).

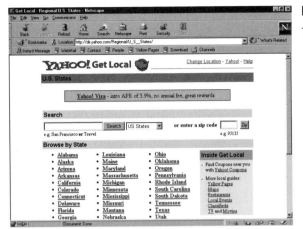

FIGURE 4-2

The U.S. States web page.

3   Click the Florida hyperlink. Yahoo! returns a web page listing a variety of hyperlinks related to Florida, including weather, news, and additional categories of information within the Florida category (see Figure 4-3).

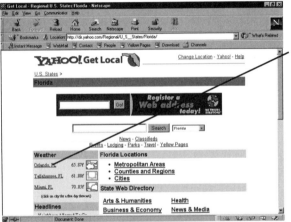

FIGURE 4-3

The Florida web page.

Click here to see the five-day weather forecast for Orlando.

4   To see more specific information about Florida, click one of the Florida web page's hyperlinks. (You might need to scroll down the web page to see all the hyperlinks.) For example, to see the five-day weather forecast for the Orlando area, click the Orlando, FL, hyperlink (see Figure 4-4).

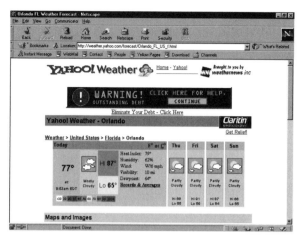

FIGURE 4-4

The five-day weather forecast for Orlando.

Although the Yahoo! search engine originally started as a directory search engine, it also works as an index search engine. To use Yahoo! as an index, enter a search term or phrase in the text box and click Search.

A directory search engine usually works best when you're searching for general information—such as information about the state of Florida. If you're looking for specific information—such as condominium rentals in Sarasota, Florida—you'll often have better luck with an index search engine.

Using an Index Search Engine

An index search engine, as mentioned previously, works much like a book's index. To use an index, you supply a term or phrase related to the information you want to find. To illustrate how this works, suppose that you want to learn more about the art of Pablo Picasso. To find information on this subject using the HotBot search engine, follow these steps:

1 Enter the URL for the HotBot search engine, *www.hotbot.com*, in the Address box provided by the web browser. Your web browser retrieves the HotBot home page (see Figure 4-5).

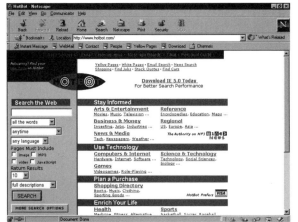

FIGURE 4-5

The main HotBot home page.

2 Type *Pablo Picasso* in the text box, and then click Search. After a few moments, the search engine returns the first page of a list of web pages that use the search term (see Figure 4-6).

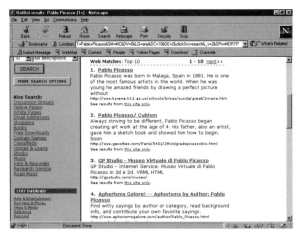

FIGURE 4-6

The search results page lists hyperlinks to web pages using the search term *Pablo Picasso.*

3 To view a listed web page, click its hyperlink. Figure 4-7, for example, shows the web page that appears after the hyperlink for the fourth Pablo Picasso web page listed is clicked.

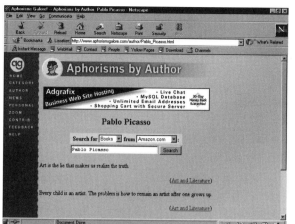

FIGURE 4-7

An example web page retrieved using the HotBot search engine.

4 To view any additional web pages that your search engine returned, click the browser's Back toolbar button until you reach the first search results web page, such as the one shown in Figure 4-6. Then repeat steps 3 and 4.

 Notes

Search engines typically return dozens and sometimes hundreds of pages of search results, but they show you only the first page of a list of web pages that most closely fit your search term. To review the next page of search results, you typically click a hyperlink at the bottom of the search results web page. The hyperlink is typically labeled something like "Next" or "Next 20 Matches." You can repeat this process until you find the information you need.

 Notes

In the previous example, the HotBot search engine was used as an index search engine, but it also works as a directory search engine, too.

Popular Search Engines

Once you understand the basic ways in which search engines work, you'll find it useful to learn the specifics about several different search engines. The remainder of this chapter describes five popular search engines with an explanation of why you might use each one and tips for fine-tuning the search engine's operation.

Using AltaVista

Although the AltaVista web site works both as an index and as a directory, this search engine's strength lies in its index.

To use the AltaVista index, follow these steps:

1 Enter *www.altavista.com* in the Address or Location box of your web browser.

2 Enter a search word or phrase in the text box provided (see Figure 4-8).

 If you enter a word or phrase in lowercase letters, AltaVista finds both uppercase and lowercase occurrences. If you enter a word or phrase in uppercase letters, AltaVista finds only occurrences that use the same uppercase lettering. In general, enter words or phrases using only lowercase letters to expand your search.

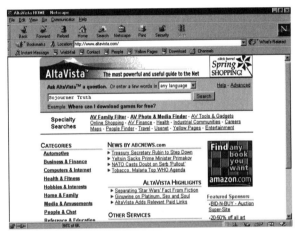

FIGURE 4-8

AltaVista supplies a rich index of web pages.

3 Click Search.

4 When AltaVista returns its list of web pages that use the word or phrase you entered in step 2, click the appropriate hyperlink (see Figure 4-9).

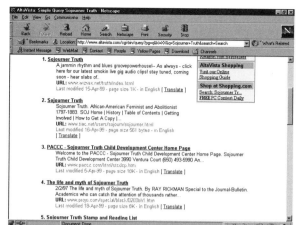

FIGURE 4-9

AltaVista returns a list of web pages that use your search term, with the best matches listed first.

You now know enough to begin working with AltaVista. However, because the AltaVista search engine returns so many results, you'll often find your searches more successful if you employ a couple of the following tricks.

- To narrow your search to web pages written in a specific language, use the Language drop-down list box to specify the language. For example, to search only web pages written in French, select French from the list box.

- If you want to find an exact word or phrase, surround it with double quotation marks. For example, to find web pages that discuss Lincoln's Gettysburg Address, enter *"Gettysburg Address"* in the search engine's text box.

- To specify that a word is either included or excluded in your search, use the plus sign (+) or the minus sign (–), preceding the characters with a space. For example, if you want to search for web pages that talk about the musician George Clinton but not President William Clinton, use the search phrase *Clinton +George –William.*

- To find occurrences of a word that can end in several different ways, use the asterisk (*) **wildcard** to stand for any set of letters. For example, if you want to find web pages that use the words *Scotland, Scots, Scottish,* and *Scotch,* enter *scot*.*

Two more tips about AltaVista will help you conduct searches in unique ways. First, AltaVista allows you to use something called a keyword. What a keyword does, in essence, is specify that you're looking for a word or phrase that is used only in a very particular way. For example, the keyword *title* lets you look for text that appears only in a web page title. To look for a web page that uses the word *Miles* in its title, enter *title:Miles* in the text box.

 For more information about which keywords AltaVista lets you use in your searches, click the Help hyperlink that appears next to the Search text box on the main AltaVista web page.

The second tip—and this won't matter to most readers—is that AltaVista also lets you use Boolean logic expressions for search operations. Boolean logic is essentially where advanced college-level mathematics meets philosophy. To use Boolean logic expressions in your searches, click the Advanced hyperlink that appears next to the Search text box on the main AltaVista web page.

Using Bigfoot

Bigfoot is a little different from the other indexes mentioned here because it's designed mainly to find people and businesses instead of web pages. You can search for a person's or a business's **e-mail** address, telephone numbers and addresses, or both. You can also use Bigfoot to search the Yellow Pages for a company's e-mail address, telephone number, and street address. To use the Bigfoot index to search for a person, follow these steps:

1 Enter *www.bigfoot.com* in the Address or Location box of your web browser.

2 Enter the person's name in the First Name box and the Last Name box.

3 Enter the city in which the person lives if you know it. Otherwise leave the City box blank.

4 Select the state in which the person lives from the drop-down list box, if you know it. Otherwise leave the State box blank.

5 Select the White Pages check box to optionally search through phone directory listings in addition to searching for e-mail addresses.

6 If you selected the White Pages check box but also want to see the e-mail listings for the person, select the EMail Addresses check box, as shown in Figure 4-10.

FIGURE 4-10

The Bigfoot Find People tab filled in.

 Bigfoot works faster if you enter as much information as possible, so if you know the city and state for the person you're searching for, enter it. If you don't find the person, leave out the city first and then the state.

7 Click Go (see Figure 4-11).

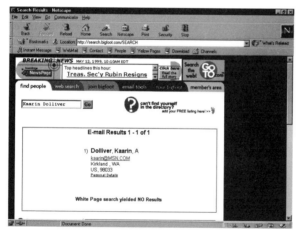

FIGURE 4-11

Bigfoot returns a list of the people it found with the name and location you specified.

That's all you need to know about Bigfoot in order to use it successfully to find someone. If you want to find a business, the procedure is slightly different. To use the Bigfoot index to search for a business, follow these steps:

1 Enter *www.bigfoot.com* in the Address or Location box of your web browser.

2 Click the Search Our Yellow Pages hyperlink.

3 To search for the business by category, choose a category from the Search By Category drop-down list box or enter a category in the Enter A Category box.

4 Enter the city for the business if you know it. Otherwise leave the City box blank.

5 Select the state in which the business is located from the drop-down list box, if you know it. Otherwise leave the State box blank.

6 Click Find It.

Notes *If you can't find yourself in Bigfoot, or the information listed about you is incorrect, you'll probably need to sign up for Bigfoot's free services to make additions or changes.*

Although most people use Bigfoot to search for people and businesses, you can also use Bigfoot to search for web pages by clicking the Web Search tab. However, you'll probably want to use the other search engines described here for any serious searching of the Web—Bigfoot's Web search engine isn't up to the same standards as search engines devoted primarily to this task.

Using HotBot

HotBot is a multifaceted search engine, offering not only an excellent index search engine but also a directory for browsing pages by category, as well as providing outstanding people- and business-finding White and Yellow Pages search engines. But HotBot's index search engine is what most people use HotBot for. With a database of more than 110 million web pages, it's one of the most thorough search engines available. The previous section, "Using an Index Search Engine," described the basics of using HotBot. This section gives you some tips to make your searches more powerful and specific.

If you enter a word or phrase in lowercase letters, HotBot finds both uppercase and lowercase occurrences. If you enter a word or phrase in uppercase letters, HotBot finds only occurrences that use the same uppercase lettering. In general, enter words or phrases using only lowercase letters to expand your search.

- HotBot by default searches for pages containing all the words you enter in the text box. If you want to broaden your search to look for any of the words you enter, select Any Of The Words from the first drop-down list box. If you want to search for an exact word or phrase, select Exact Phrase from the first drop-down list box. You can also search for a page with a specific title, or you can use Boolean expressions by selecting the appropriate entry from the first drop-down list box.

- To search for recently created pages only, select a time frame from the second drop-down list box.

- To narrow your search to web pages written in a specific language, select a language from the third drop-down list box.

- To search for pages including only images, videos, MP3 sounds, or JavaScript, select the appropriate check box.

- To specify that a word is either included in or excluded from your search, use the plus sign (+) or the minus sign (–), preceding the characters with a space. For example, if you want to search for web pages that talk about the musician George Clinton but not President William Clinton, enter the search phrase *Clinton +George –William.*

- To find occurrences of a word that can end in several different ways, use the asterisk (*) wildcard to stand for any set of letters. For example, if you want to find web pages that use the words *Scotland, Scots, Scottish,* and *Scotch,* enter *scot*.*

You can also search HotBot with something called a meta word, or keyword. Meta words let you search a web page for information other than that presented in the text. For example, you can use the title meta word to search for words that appear only in a web page's title. To look for a web page that uses the word *Europa* in its title, enter *title:Europa* in the text box. There are lots of other meta words you can use, such as ones to search for pages only at specific domain names or for pages containing only certain types of plug-ins.

 For more information about all of HotBot's advanced search capabilities, click the Help button located at the top of the HotBot home page and then click the Search Tips hyperlink.

Using Lycos

Like AltaVista and HotBot, Lycos works both as an index and as a directory, but this search engine's strength lies in its index. To use Lycos's index, follow these steps:

1 Enter *www.lycos.com* in the Address or Location box of your web browser.

2 Enter a search word or phrase in the text box provided (see Figure 4-12).

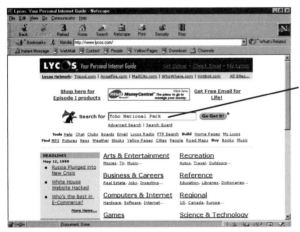

FIGURE 4-12

Lycos can find a large number of pages on virtually any subject.

The Search For text box.

3 Click Go Get It!

4 When Lycos returns its list of web pages that use the word or phrase you entered in step 2, click the appropriate hyperlink (see Figure 4-13).

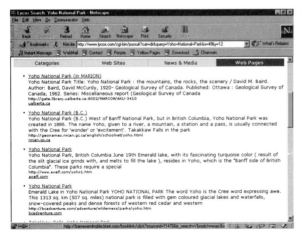

FIGURE 4-13

Lycos returns a list of web pages that use your search term, with the best matches listed first.

You now know enough to begin searching the web with Lycos, although if you want to perform more advanced searches, here are a couple of tricks you can try, most of which also work on the other search engines.

- If you want to find an exact word or phrase, surround it with double quotation marks. For example, to find web pages that discuss Lincoln's Gettysburg Address, enter *"Gettysburg Address"* in the search engine's text box.

- To specify that a word is either included in or excluded from your search, use the plus sign (+) or the minus sign (–), preceding the characters with a space. For example, if you want to search for web pages that talk about the musician George Clinton but not President William Clinton, enter the search phrase *Clinton +George –William.*

- To find occurrences of a word that can end in several different ways, use the asterisk (*) wildcard to stand for any set of letters. For example, if you want to find web pages that use the words *Scotland, Scots, Scottish,* and *Scotch,* enter *scot*.*

You can also click the Advanced Search hyperlink (located in the lower left of the Lycos home page) to access the Advanced Search web page, as shown in Figure 4-14.

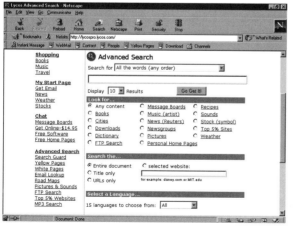

FIGURE 4-14

The Advanced Search web page.

Use this page to conduct more sophisticated searches using many additional options:

- Lycos by default searches for pages containing all the words you enter in the text box. If you want to broaden your search to look for any of the words you enter, select Any Of The Words from the Search For drop-down list box. If you want to search for an exact word or phrase, select The Exact Phrase from the Search For drop-down list box. You can also search for a page with a specific title or search by using the plus (+) and minus (–) signs described earlier with the appropriate entry from the Search For drop-down list box.

- To search using a natural language query, select Natural Language Query from the Search For drop-down list box.

- To search for books, pictures, recipes, or another specific type of page, click the appropriate option button in the Look For section.

- To narrow your search to web pages written in a specific language, select a language from the Select A Language drop-down list box.

Using Yahoo!

Yahoo! is different from the other search engines described in this chapter. Instead of having a computer-organized, mostly comprehensive database of all the web pages on the Internet, Yahoo! maintains a relatively select directory of web pages that have been categorized by people. The advantage of a directory like Yahoo! is that not only can it be easier to locate what you want if you don't know the right keywords, but also the quality of sites in the directory is generally higher than that in the comprehensive databases of index search engines, which might contain a large number of duplicate links or incomplete pages. On the other hand, since Yahoo! relies on people to keep their indexes current, their search results are slightly more out of date.

The most common way to find information with Yahoo! is to browse the directory by category. The directory structure of Yahoo! is particularly useful when you're interested in getting a feel for what's available on the Web. Rather than search for a very specific topic, you can browse general categories looking for a page that interests you. Although Yahoo!'s directory is much smaller than the database for an index search engine, it still contains links to more than 500,000 sites in 25,000 categories, which makes browsing cumbersome sometimes. For this reason, you can also perform a standard, index-style search of the Yahoo! directory, giving you some of the advantages of both types of search engines. To browse the Yahoo! directory, follow these steps:

1 Enter *www.yahoo.com* in the Address or Location box of your web browser.

2 Click the broad category in which you want to find a page.

3 When Yahoo! displays a list of subcategories, click a category to display a deeper list of categories, or eventually, a list of related web pages (see Figure 4-15).

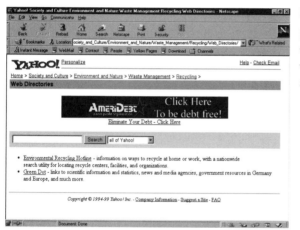

FIGURE 4-15

Browsing Yahoo! is a great way to find information if you're not looking for a specific web page.

4 Click the web site hyperlink you want to1 visit to go to that site.

To search the Yahoo! directory, follow these steps:

1 Enter *www.yahoo.com* in the Address or Location box of your web browser.

2 Enter the word or phrase you want to search for in the text box provided.

3 Click Search.

4 Yahoo! then displays a list of categories and web pages that match your search. Click a category listing to browse the category, or click a web page listing to go to that page (see Figure 4-16).

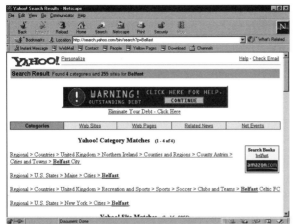

FIGURE 4-16

When you search the Yahoo! directory, you see a list of categories and pages that match your search criteria.

That's pretty much all there is to using Yahoo! to find information on the Web. However, like the rest of the search engines available, Yahoo! does offer advanced searching capabilities. To use these advanced search capabilities, click the Advanced Search hyperlink or simply use some of the following pointers when entering your search words.

- If you want to find an exact word or phrase, surround it with double quotation marks. For example, to find web pages that discuss Lincoln's Gettysburg Address, enter *"Gettysburg Address"* in the search engine's text box.

- To specify that a word is either included in or excluded from your search, use the plus sign (+) or the minus sign (–), preceding the characters with a space. For example, if you want to search for web pages that talk about the musician George Clinton but not President William Clinton, enter the search phrase *Clinton +George –William.*

- To find occurrences of a word that can end in several different ways, use the asterisk (*) wildcard to stand for any set of letters. For example, if you want to find web pages that use the words *Scotland, Scots, Scottish,* and *Scotch,* enter *scot*.*

CHAPTER 5

Popular Places to Visit on the Web

The previous chapters described the basics of how to navigate the **World Wide Web** and find what you're looking for. This chapter gives you a rundown of the most popular World Wide Web activities to give you a head start as you begin exploring the Web. This chapter covers the following topics:

- Researching purchases
- Accessing local information
- Getting the latest news
- Shopping

 Web sites *change frequently, so the specific steps described here or the appearance of a particular web site might be a little different by the time you read this. But even if there are changes, the instructions and descriptions in this chapter should give you a basic idea of how to use a major web site. And when there are changes, they usually make finding the information that you need easier.*

Researching Purchases

The World Wide Web is perhaps the best place to find consumer information. It contains a wealth of government, nonprofit, and commercial web sites that you can browse to find ratings, prices, and customer commentary on just about any product. So before you make any important purchase, you probably want to check out the World Wide Web to compare prices and verify customer satisfaction for the item you want to buy.

*The web sites listed in this chapter are not the only web sites with good information on each topic. You can use the **search engines** that you learned about in Chapter 4 to find other excellent web sites.*

Buying a Vehicle

Before buying a new or used vehicle, you can investigate the vehicle's safety and reliability ratings. Two of the most popular web sites for automobile information are Edmund's Automobile Buyer's Guide at *http://www.edmunds.com*, as shown in Figure 5-1, and Microsoft CarPoint at *http://www.carpoint.msn.com*.

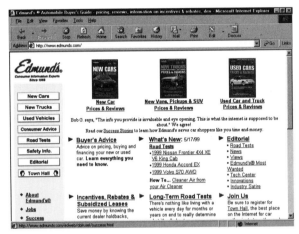

FIGURE 5-1

Edmund's Automobile Buyer's Guide.

For government information, including crash tests and recalls, turn to the National Highway Traffic Safety Administration (NHTSA) site at *http://www.nhtsa.do⁺.gov*, as shown in Figure 5-2.

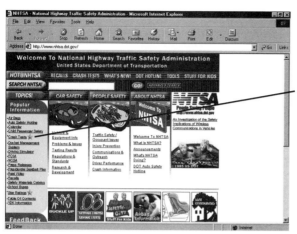

FIGURE 5-2

The National Highway Traffic Safety Administration home page.

Click the Crash Tests hyperlink to see how your vehicle or the vehicle you intend to purchase performed in NHTSA crash tests.

To see whether an automobile manufacturer has recalled any defective parts on your current car or the car you intend to buy, follow these steps:

1 Click the Recalls **hyperlink** at the top of the page or in the list at the left.

2 Click the Recall Searches By Make, Model, Year hyperlink.

3 Choose a year from the Year drop-down list box on the left, and click Submit Year.

4 On the next page your browser displays, select a make from the Make drop-down list box, and click Submit Make.

5 On the next page your browser displays, select a model from the Model drop-down list box, and click Submit Model.

6 Leave the Type Of Component drop-down list box blank, and click Submit Make, Model And Year Query. This displays a list of all parts recalled by the manufacturer for the make, model, and year of the vehicle you chose (see Figure 5-3). The list also contains phone numbers you can call if a dealer refuses to correct or replace the malfunctioning part within a reasonable amount of time.

FIGURE 5-3

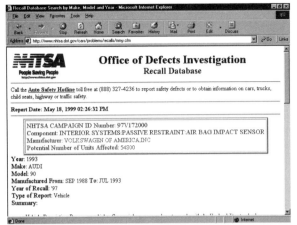

The Insurance Institute for Highway Safety conducts some crash tests of its own, and you can find the results at *http://www.hwysafety.org*.

For automobile pricing information, visit the Kelley Blue Book web site at *http://www.kbb.com*.

The Bureau of Automotive Repair Consumer's Guide to Buying a Used Car by the State of California Department of Consumer Affairs at *http://smogcheck.ca.gov/cpo/100016.htm* also has a thorough checklist for buying a used car, as well as a list of other governmental agencies you may need or want to turn to when purchasing a vehicle.

Buying a House

If you're looking to buy a home, visit *http://www.realtor.com*, the National Association of Realtors' web site. You can gather information here and browse homes listed by Realtors on the Multiple Listing Service, as shown in Figure 5-4.

FIGURE 5-4

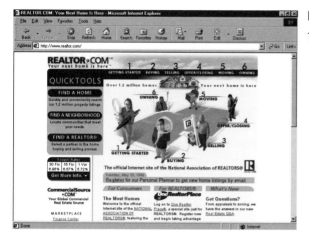

To browse listings in your area, follow these steps:

1 Click the Find A Home hyperlink.

2 Click a state on the map.

3 Click a region on the map. (Or click one of the region hyperlinks.)

4 Click a county hyperlink.

5 Select a community from the list, and click Continue. If you want to select multiple communities, hold down the Ctrl key as you select them.

6 Enter the information about price range, number of bedrooms and bathrooms, and square footage, and click Find Home.

Notes *While you can select more specific options, remember that the data is only as good as the data entry skills and specificity of the people who entered it in their computers. You can often find a home that you like with the options that you want when you keep your search more general.*

7 For some listings, you can see where homes are located. If you see a Map Home hyperlink, you can click it to see exactly where a home is located.

You can also see whether a real estate agency in your area has a web site. If you already have a Realtor checking the Multiple Listing Service for you, you may want to spend your time checking homes for sale by owner. The Freehomelistings.com (*http://www.freehomelistings.com*) and Owners.com (*http://www.owners.com*) web sites have nationwide listings and are good places to start looking. You may also want to use a search engine to conduct a search of homes for sale in your state or region.

Homefair.com (*http://www2.homefair.com*) has a wealth of neighborhood and consumer information, as well as tools you can use to calculate moving costs and determine the housing price range you can afford. You may also find Fannie Mae's HomePath at *http://www.homepath.com* a useful tool in stepping you through the process of financing and purchasing a home.

 Notes If you're looking for rental properties, two good sites to visit are AllApartments at http://www.allapartments.com *and Rent.Net at* http://www.rent.net.

When it comes to arranging the financing, you can research and even apply for mortgages online. For information about current mortgage rates in your area, check out Bankrate.com at *http://www.bankrate.com* (see Figure 5-5). Homeowners.com at *http://www.homeowners.com* is also a great site for mortgage information.

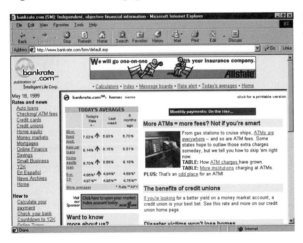

FIGURE 5-5

The Bankrate.com web site.

 To find an ATM wherever you are, you can use either the MasterCard/Cirrus or VISA ATM Locator sites at http://www.mastercard.com/atm *and* http://www.visa.com.

General Consumer Information

For information about other consumer products, you can use a search engine (as described in Chapter 4) or visit company web sites directly. For information about product recalls and other consumer safety issues, see the Consumer Product Safety Commission (CPSC) web site at *http://www.cpsc.gov*. If you click the Recalls:News hyperlink, and then click the Latest Recalls hyperlink, your **web browser** displays a **web page** similar to the one shown in Figure 5-6. You can search the database of recalls by date, topic, or specific product.

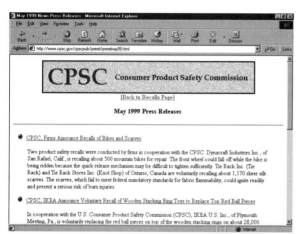

FIGURE 5-6

The latest recalls announced by the CPSC.

For ratings information on several products, visit *Consumer Reports* **online** at *http://www.consumerreports.org*.

Notes: To access several areas of the Consumer Reports *site, you must pay a subscription fee. Many web sites require payment for some of the information the site has available. Another example of a "pay" web site is the* Wall Street Journal *at* http://www.wsj.com. *Membership organizations such as labor unions often require you to be up to date with your membership fees before allowing you access to their web sites. In any case, when you pay, the organization gives you a user name and* **password** *to allow access.*

Before you support a company with your business or donate money to a charity, you may want to do a background check on the organization by visiting the Better Business Bureau web site at *http://www.bbb.org*.

Accessing Local Information

Despite the expanse of the World Wide Web, it can help you find local information just as well as it can help you find international information. You can visit web sites that inform you of local weather, driving conditions, and events, as well as sites that map out the area you choose.

Weather and Driving Conditions

For the official information on driving conditions, including road closures, construction, and often traffic reports, refer to the appropriate state Department of Transportation. You can access a web page listing the Departments of Transportation by state for 39 of the states using Yahoo! Just click the Business & Economy category hyperlink, click the Transportation hyperlink, click the Government Agencies hyperlink, click the United States hyperlink, and click the State Departments Of Transportation hyperlink.

Figure 5-7 shows the Puget Sound Area Traffic Cameras web page on the Washington State Department of Transportation web site.

FIGURE 5-7

Pictures of traffic flow in the Puget Sound area.

For current local weather conditions and national forecasts, access The Weather Channel at *http://www.weather.com*, Intellicast weather at *http://www.intellicast.com/weather/usa/*, or AccuWeather at *http://www.accuweather.com*.

Maps

If you need a map or driving directions for an area, check out MapQuest at *http://www.mapquest.com*. Just click the Maps hyperlink, enter the street address you're looking for in the text boxes (see Figure 5-8), and click Get Map to have MapQuest return a map of the address you requested, as shown in Figure 5-9.

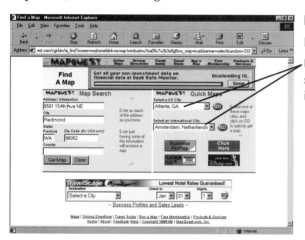

FIGURE 5-8

Mapping an address.

Use these dialog boxes to see maps of entire cities instead.

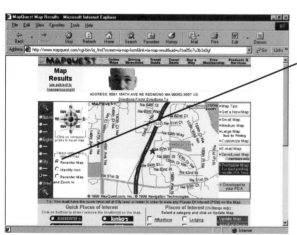

FIGURE 5-9

The map of an address.

Click these option buttons to zoom in or out or recenter the map.

Other sources for maps are Expedia Maps at *http://www.expediamaps.com* and MapBlast! at *http://www.mapblast.com*.

Getting the Latest News

You can wait until the evening news or the morning paper to find out about current events, or if you have an **Internet** connection, you can inform yourself of breaking news within minutes of when it occurs. Many popular newspapers and magazines now publish their content online.

Headline News

Several newspapers publish their content online so that you can read the latest news before the newspaper ever arrives at your house. One of the best parts of online newspapers is that most don't require a subscription. Another benefit of news in electronic form is that you can easily search the content for exactly the information you need. So instead of spending an hour looking through the furniture classifieds for a full-size mattress, you can enter a search term and read only the advertisements that interest you. Table 5-1 lists the national and local newspapers with the largest circulations and where you can find them on the Internet.

Newspaper	URL
Boston Globe	http://www.boston.com/globe/
Chicago Tribune	http://chicagotribune.com/
Christian Science Monitor	http://www.csmonitor.com
Dallas Morning News	http://www.dallasnews.com/
Detroit Free Press	http://www.freep.com/
Houston Chronicle	http://www.chron.com/
Los Angeles Times	http://www.latimes.com/
New York Daily News	http://www.nydailynews.com
New York Newsday	http://www.newsday.com/
New York Times	http://www.nytimes.com/
Philadelphia Enquirer	http://www.phillynews.com/inq/
USA Today	http://www.usatoday.com/
Washington Post	http://www.washingtonpost.com/

TABLE 5-1: Online newspapers.

Several popular magazines also have online editions, many of which you can browse without purchasing a subscription. Table 5-2 lists some popular magazines and where you can find them online.

Magazine	URL
Cosmopolitan	*http://cosmomag.com/*
Country Living	*http://homearts.com/cl/toc/00clhpc1.htm*
Field & Stream	*http://www.fieldandstream.com/*
Glamour	*http://www.swoon.com/mag_rack/glamour.html*
Good Housekeeping	*http://homearts.com/gh/toc/00ghhpc1.htm*
Ladies' Home Journal	*http://www.lhj.com/*
Life	*http://pathfinder.com/life*
Motorland	*http://www.csaa.com/travel/feaarticles-trvser*
National Enquirer	*http://www.nationalenquirer.com/*
National Geographic	*http://www.nationalgeographic.com/*
People	*http://pathfinder.com/people*
Popular Mechanics	*http://popularmechanics.com*
Popular Science	*http://www.popsci.com/*
Reader's Digest	*http://www.readersdigest.com*
Redbook	*http://homearts.com/rb/toc/00rbhpc1.htm*
Smithsonian	*http://www.smithsonianmag.si.edu/*
Time	*http://pathfinder.com/time*
U.S. News & World Report	*http://www.usnews.com/*

TABLE 5-2: Online magazines.

Sports

Although you can get sports updates on several news web sites, a couple of web sites specialize in sports, so you can read all the details and track events and commentary that might not make it into the sports sections of other Web sources. Visit *Sports Illustrated* at *http://pathfinder.com/si* or ESPN at *http://ESPNET.SportsZone.com/*. Figure 5-10 shows the rugby **home page** on the *Sports Illustrated* web site.

Rugby fans can get all the news on the *Sports Illustrated* web site.

For specific sports, you can visit the sport organization's official site. Table 5-3 lists some official web sites for popular sports.

Association	Address
MLB	*http://www.majorleaguebaseball.com*
Nascar	*http://www.nascar.com*
NBA	*http://www.nba.com*
NFL	*http://www.nfl.com*
NHL	*http://www.nhl.com*
PGA	*http://www.pga.com*
WNBA	*http://www.wnba.com*

TABLE 5-3: Sports associations online.

Entertainment and Broadcast Media

Numerous television stations publish their schedules and information from their programs on the World Wide Web. Table 5-4 lists the **URLs** for the major television networks.

Network	URL
ABC	http://www.abcnews.com
CBS	http://www.cbs.com
CNN	http://www.cnn.com
Fox	http://www.foxnetwork.com
MSNBC	http://www.msnbc.com
NBC	http://www.nbc.com
NPR	http://www.npr.org/
PBS	http://www.pbs.org/
UPN	http://www.upn.com
WB	http://www.thewb.com/

TABLE 5-4: Television networks online.

For television listings, there's *TV Guide* at *http://www.tvguide.com*.

 Notes *Windows 98 comes with a feature called WebTV for Windows that allows you to watch broadcast or cable TV on your computer. To use this feature, you need to have a hardware device called a TV tuner card installed on your computer.*

If you're looking for information about movies, visit the Internet Movie Database at *http://www.imdb.com*.

To access a wealth of local information and event news for about 75 of the larger cities in the United States, check out a Sidewalk web site. To go to the Sidewalk web site for a particular city, enter *http://national.sidewalk.msn.com* in the Address or Location box of your browser and then click the Click Here To Choose A City hyperlink to enter or select a city. Or you can also enter the name of a city followed by *sidewalk.com* to go directly to that city's web site. For example, to visit Seattle Sidewalk, type *http://seattle.sidewalk.com* to open the home page (see Figure 5-11).

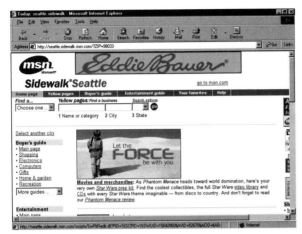

FIGURE 5-11

The home page for Seattle Sidewalk.

To purchase tickets for events nationwide, visit the Ticketmaster web site at *http://www.ticketmaster.com.*

Business

Investors can access several types of information online. For the latest business news, both *Money* magazine's web site at *http://pathfinder.com/money* and the *Wall Street Journal* web site at *http://www.wsj.com/* specialize in business news and information.

You can also visit the Nasdaq home page at *http://www.nasdaq.com/* or the New York Stock Exchange at *http://www.nyse.com/.*

Several web sites allow you to trade online, such as Charles Schwab at *http://www.schwab.com,* Datek at *http://www.datek.com,* E*Trade at *http://www.etrade.com,* and Waterhouse Securities at *http://www.waterhouse.com.*

You can access financial information and other information about publicly traded securities at the Securities and Exchange Commission (SEC) web site. The SEC is the regulatory agency responsible for administering federal securities laws, and you can visit its web site at *http://www.sec.gov.* You can also access information about public and private companies at Companies Online at *http://www.companiesonline.com* or Hoover's Online at *http://www.hoovers.com.* For a comprehensive source of general personal-finance information and links to hundreds of other personal finance sources, visit the web site for the popular software program Quicken at *http://www.quicken.com.*

If you own a small business, you'll find the U.S. Small Business Administration web site at *http://www.sba.gov* a gateway to several business resources, both private and governmental. The web page at *http://www.sba.gov/world/federal-servers.html* lists countless federal resources useful to businesses.

Shopping

The Internet has some good buys for several products and services you might want to purchase. Some of the most popular types of shopping on the Internet are travel reservations and purchases; books, music, and software; and auctions.

Travel

You can often find good deals on the World Wide Web for travel, including airline tickets, cruises, car rentals, and lodging. You can research the cost of a trip, make travel arrangements, and pay for the arrangements all in one stop at the Microsoft Expedia web site at *http://www.expedia.msn.com.*

To quickly see flight information and prices, enter the cities, dates, and time of day for your outgoing and returning flights and the number of adults traveling, as shown in Figure 5-12. Then click Go.

FIGURE 5-12

Searching for best-priced flights.

Click these hyperlinks to search for and reserve accommodations or rental cars.

If Expedia can't find a match for one of the cities you entered, perhaps because that city has more than one airport, select the desired airport from the drop-down list box on the next web page and click Continue. After Expedia finishes searching for flights that meet your criteria, it lists them in ascending order of price, as shown in Figure 5-13.

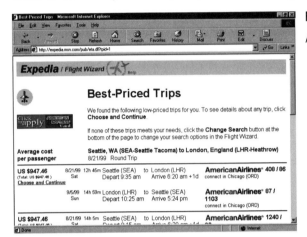

FIGURE 5-13

Available flights.

To select a flight, click the Choose And Continue hyperlink. Expedia displays the details of the flight. Follow the instructions onscreen for booking and paying for the flight if you choose to do so.

Other web sites such as Cheap Tickets at *http:/www.cheaptickets.com/*, Preview Travel at *http://www.previewtravel.com*, and Travelocity at *http://www.travelocity.com* offer similar services.

Before you travel to a foreign country, especially a developing country, be sure to check out the Centers for Disease Control web site at *http://www.cdc.gov*. It lists health warnings and offers guidelines for keeping healthy abroad. Read any travel warnings from the State Department at *http://travel.state.gov*.

You can also check out the web sites for individual airlines. Many airlines, such as Southwest, offer Internet specials on their web sites. Others, such as Alaska, offer numerous deals for last-minute flights. Table 5-5 lists large U.S. airlines and their addresses on the World Wide Web.

Airline	URL
Alaska	*http://www.alaskaair.com*
American	*http://www.aa.com*
Continental	*http://www.continental.com*
Delta	*http://www.delta-air.com*
Hawaiian	*http://www.hawaiianair.com*
Horizon	*http://www.horizonair.com*
Northwest	*http://www.nwa.com*
Southwest	*http://www.southwest.com*
TWA	*http://www.twa.com*
United	*http://www.ual.com*
US Airways	*http://www.usairways.com*

TABLE 5-5: U.S. airlines on the web.

For train travel, check out Amtrak's web site at http://www.amtrak.com. *For bus travel, visit Greyhound's site at* http://www.greyhound.com.

Books, Music, and Computer Products

To browse and purchase books, music, and software, go to the Barnes & Noble web site at *http://www.barnesandnoble.com.* To search for a specific book, use the convenient Quick Search tool. Select Title, Author, or Keyword from the drop-down list box and enter the text in the text box below. Then click Search. Your web browser displays a list of books that meet your criteria, such as those shown in Figure 5-14.

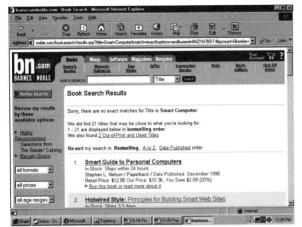

FIGURE 5-14

The Barnes & Noble web site allows you to search for a specific book.

For information and reviews about computers and computer software and hardware, look to ZDNet, home of several popular computing magazines, at *http://www.zdnet.com*. Or visit CNET at *http://www.cnet.com*. Both sites also have **shareware** and freeware that you can **download.** Figure 5-15 shows the Downloads page at the ZDNet web site.

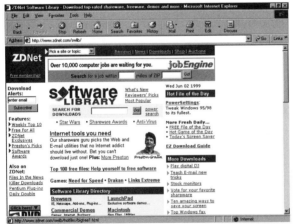

FIGURE 5-15

Downloading freeware and shareware from ZDNet.

To purchase computers, computer hardware, and computer software, go to CDW at *http://www.cdw.com*, CompUSA at *http://www.compusa.com*, or MicroWarehouse at *http://www.warehouse.com,* to name a few.

Table 5-6 lists the web sites of the nation's largest computer manufacturers.

Manufacturer	URL
Apple	http://www.apple.com
Compaq	http://www.compaq.com
Dell	http://www.dell.com
Hewlett-Packard	http://www.hp.com
IBM	http://www.ibm.com
Packard Bell	http://www.packardbell.com/

TABLE 5-6: Computer manufacturers online.

Auctions

You can buy or sell collectibles and other items at online auctions. Probably the most popular online auction house is eBay at *http://www.ebay.com*, where you can browse through items by category and subcategory. At eBay you'll find a brief description of the item, along with the highest bid, the number of bids placed, and the date and time the auction for that item ends. Click an item to read a detailed description and often see a picture of that item. Another way to browse eBay is by entering a keyword and searching for specific items (see Figure 5-16).

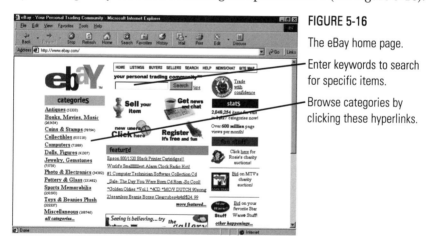

FIGURE 5-16

The eBay home page.

Enter keywords to search for specific items.

Browse categories by clicking these hyperlinks.

If you bid on an item or submit an item for auction on eBay, you are making a legally binding commitment to purchase or sell the item in question. If this is not your intent, do not actually enter the information from this book in your browser.

To bid on an item, scroll down to the Bidding area at the bottom of the item's description and follow these steps:

1 Enter the maximum you are willing to pay for the item.

2 Click Review Bid.

3 Enter your user ID and your password. (You create these terms when you register.)

4 Click Place Bid, and eBay raises the current bid by the current bid increment and continues to top any other bids by the bid increment until the auction is over or your maximum price is exceeded. In this way you don't need to keep outbidding other bidders until the auction ends.

To sell an item, click Sell Your Item on the eBay home page. Figure 5-17 shows the **form** you use to list an item.

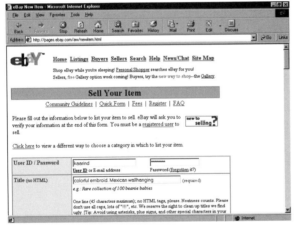

FIGURE 5-17

Selling an item at eBay.

To fill out the form, follow these steps:

1 Enter your user ID and password.

2 Enter a short, descriptive title for your item.

3 Specify the location of the item.

4 Select the category under which you want eBay to list the item.

5 Enter a description of the item.

6 Optionally, if you've published a picture of the item on the World Wide Web, enter the picture's URL. In most cases, you can publish pictures for eBay auctions using the web site space provided with your **ISP** membership fees. But this depends on the rules of your ISP.

7 Enter the quantity you are selling.

8 Enter the lowest price at which you'd be willing to sell the item.

9 Select a time limit for the auction from the Duration drop-down list box.

5

CHAPTER 6

Using E-Mail

One of the most popular features of the **Internet** is electronic mail, or **e-mail** for short. The popularity of e-mail is easy to understand. It allows for communication across vast distances, it's fast, and it's inexpensive. When you correspond using the Internet, you can send messages across the world, they arrive in the blink of an eye, and it costs next to nothing to send as many as you care to write. All you need is an Internet connection and some software that you can get for free. This chapter describes how to use **Microsoft Outlook Express** and **Netscape Messenger**, two free, easy-to-use e-mail programs, by covering the following topics:

- How e-mail works
- Setting up your computer for e-mail
- Using Outlook Express for e-mail
- Using Netscape Messenger for e-mail

 *You don't need to use Outlook Express or Netscape Messenger for your electronic correspondence. Another good e-mail program is **Eudora**. You can **download** a free copy of Eudora at* http://www.eudora.com. *Alternately, common e-mail programs in the corporate world work just as well for sending messages through the Internet, as long as your company **network** is connected. Two examples are Profs and cc:Mail.*

 You can also get a free e-mail account from a number of companies such as Hotmail (http://www.hotmail.com) *and USA.net* (http:// www.usa.net). *You can then either use their **web pages** to work with your e-mail or, in some cases, use an e-mail program such as Outlook Express that can work with Web-based e-mail.*

 Chapter 2 describes how to set up an Internet connection, which is a prerequisite to working with e-mail.

How E-Mail Works

E-mail works like this: Using a program such as Outlook Express or Netscape Messenger, you create a message and then tell your e-mail program to send the message to your e-mail post office (which, technically, is called a mail **server**). Your e-mail post office then sends the message to the recipient's e-mail post office (technically, another mail server). The next time the recipient's e-mail **client** "visits" the e-mail post office and checks his or her mailbox, the recipient receives the e-mail message.

 E-mail programs are often called e-mail clients.

Before you can send someone an e-mail message, you need to know the person's e-mail name and address. This e-mail name and address identifies both the person you're sending the message to and, in essence, the mail server that the person uses to pick up his or her e-mail messages. An example demonstrates how simple this process is.

 To be precise, you don't actually have to know the name of the recipient's mail server. You need to know only the name of the domain of the network of computers the person uses to connect to the Internet.

Suppose you want to send a message to the president of the United States. To do this, you need to know the **domain name** that the White House uses for its e-mail and you need to know the e-mail name that the White House uses to identify the president's e-mail mailbox. It turns out that the president's full e-mail name and address is *president@whitehouse.gov.* So the president's e-mail name is "president," and the White House domain name is "whitehouse.gov." The e-mail name and the domain name are separated by the "@" symbol.

Notes *When someone verbally gives an e-mail name and address, they say "at" in place of the @ symbol and "dot" in place of a period. So to describe the president's e-mail name and address, say "president at whitehouse dot gov." Note, however, that the actual e-mail name and address you type is* president@whitehouse.gov.

That's all you need to know to understand and use e-mail. Figure 6-1 shows a simple e-mail message created using Outlook Express.

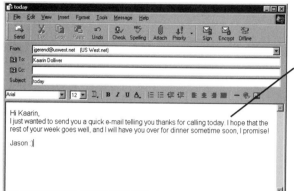

FIGURE 6-1

Most e-mail messages are short text messages.

This is the message text.

Notes *Many companies and organizations use mailing lists to e-mail information, such as newsletters, to large groups of people. Some mailing lists are public, others are private. How you join a mailing list depends on the way in which the sponsor set it up. You might fill out a form on a **web site** to join a mailing list. You might send a specific message to a mailing list server to add your name to a list. Typically, this process is automated, so the message must contain certain elements in certain parts of the message, such as the word SUBSCRIBE in the message subject and nothing else. Or your name might be automatically placed on a mailing list when you give your e-mail address to an organization. To see a list of public mailing lists and the instructions for joining them, visit the web site at http://www.liszt.com. You'll probably receive weekly or even daily messages from the mailing lists that you join, so be prudent about how many lists you sign up for.*

Setting Up A Computer for E-Mail

Before you can begin enjoying the benefits of e-mail, you need to set up the computer for e-mail. This process involves a couple of steps. First, you need to make sure that you have an e-mail program such as Outlook Express or Netscape Messenger (part of **Netscape Communicator**). If you have already installed Internet Explorer or Netscape Communicator, you almost surely have installed Outlook Express or Netscape Messenger as a part of the process. Then you need to set up an e-mail account.

Notes You can send and receive e-mail from any computer that is connected to the Internet and provides an e-mail client. You do, however, need to follow the steps described here for setting up the computer.

If you're running **Microsoft Windows** 98 or Windows 2000, Outlook Express is almost surely installed and ready to go on your computer. If, on the other hand, you're running Windows 95, you may need to install Internet Explorer in order to use Outlook Express. Outlook Express installs by default when you install Internet Explorer.

If you want to use Netscape Messenger, you need to have Netscape Communicator installed on your computer. If this didn't come with your Internet connection software, you can download it for free from Netscape's web site at *http://www.netscape.com.*

To be able to send and receive e-mail messages, your e-mail client needs to know a little about you. For instance, it needs to know the name of your electronic "post office," or mail server. It also needs to know the name of your mailbox. If you have an account with a large **ISP**, such as America Online, AT&T WorldNet, CompuServe, or the Microsoft Network, the ISP's software sets up your e-mail account for you. The first time you access your e-mail client, you also often start a **wizard** that steps you through a series of dialog boxes to provide the client with the information it needs. If you don't know what to enter in one of the wizard's dialog boxes, contact your ISP.

Notes If you used the **Internet Connection Wizard** in Chapter 2 to set up an ISP account, you were asked to include the "Incoming Mail" and "Outgoing Mail" server information.

Using Outlook Express for E-Mail

After you install and set up an e-mail client, you're ready to begin using e-mail. This section describes how to use Outlook Express to accomplish the most important e-mailing tasks: reading e-mail messages, creating and delivering e-mail messages, building a list of e-mail **contacts**, replying to and forwarding e-mail messages, deleting e-mail messages, and attaching files to messages. Keep in mind that you don't need to use Outlook Express as your e-mail client. Netscape Messenger is covered later in this chapter, but you can also use other e-mail clients to accomplish these same tasks. The steps for doing so vary only slightly.

Notes Outlook Express version 5 is used throughout this section. If you have an older or newer version, features may look and work slightly differently from what is described here, but the overall feel will be very similar.

 Notes Outlook Express contains a subset of the features in a related product that comes with Microsoft Office called **Microsoft Outlook.** Outlook contains additional features for scheduling appointments and events, keeping a journal of activities, and recording tasks. If you use the full version of Outlook, you'll find that many of the steps described here for working with e-mail are very similar to the steps in Outlook. If you're used to working with Outlook, you can make Outlook Express work and look a little more like Outlook by choosing the View menu's Layout command and selecting the Outlook Bar check box.

Reading E-Mail Messages

To read your e-mail messages in Outlook Express, start the program by either clicking its icon on the Quick Launch toolbar next to the Start button or by clicking the Start button, choosing Programs, and then clicking Outlook Express. After you start Outlook Express, click the Inbox folder. Outlook Express lists your messages in the Folder Contents pane and shows a message in the Preview pane, as shown in Figure 6-2.

6

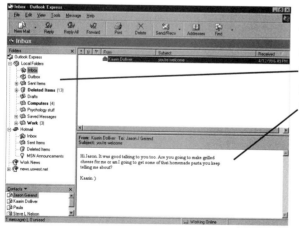

FIGURE 6-2

The Outlook Express program window.

This is the Folder Contents pane.

This is the Preview pane.

To check for new messages, click the Send And Receive toolbar button. (Depending on the display settings for your monitor, this toolbar button might be abbreviated Send/Recv.)

 Notes *When you start Outlook Express, Windows might display the Connect To dialog box so you can connect to the Internet. If this happens, you can click Connect to retrieve new messages immediately. You can also choose to connect later, so you can read messages you've already downloaded or create new messages before connecting.*

If you want to open a new window especially for a message—perhaps so you can see more of the message—double-click the message in the Folder Contents pane. Outlook Express opens a window for the message. After you read the message, click the Close button.

 If you're using the full version of Outlook, click Inbox on the Outlook bar and click the Send/Receive toolbar button to receive new messages.

Creating E-Mail Messages

To create an e-mail message using Outlook Express, follow these steps:

1 Click the New Mail toolbar button to display the New Message window, as shown in Figure 6-3.

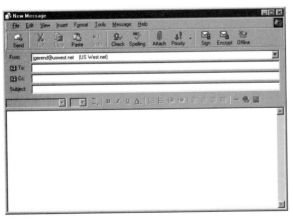

FIGURE 6-3

A blank New Message window.

To create a new message in the full version of Outlook, click Inbox on the Outlook bar and click the New toolbar button.

2 Enter the e-mail name of the message recipient in the To box.

 You can send a message or message copy to more than one recipient. To do this, enter e-mail names separated by semicolons.

3 Type a brief description of your message's subject in the Subject box.

4 Type your message in the large text box. Figure 6-4 shows a partial message.

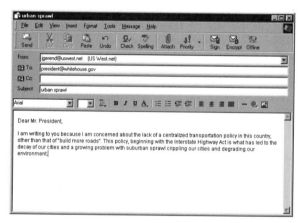

FIGURE 6-4

A partial message.

5 Optionally, use the Message window's formatting toolbar buttons to format your message.

 *To properly view your message, the message recipient must use an e-mail client program (like Outlook Express or Netscape Messenger) that understands how to display any formatting you apply. For this reason, it's often best to format your message in Plain Text if you don't know the kind of e-mail program your recipient uses. To do this, choose the Format menu's Plain Text command. To always send messages in Plain Text format to a particular person, open the person's **Address Book** entry, click the Name tab, and then select the Send E-Mail Using Plain Text Only check box.*

To check the spelling in your message, click the Spelling button in your toolbar. If Outlook Express finds an incorrectly spelled word, it displays a dialog box in which you can correct the misspelling.

6 If you have set up more than one e-mail account, you can select the e-mail account you want to use by clicking the Down arrow in the From line.

7 After you finish typing your message, click the Send toolbar button to place the message in your Outbox folder. After you click Send, Windows might display the Connect To dialog box to ask whether it should connect you to the Internet so you can send the message. If you want to connect, click Connect.

 Notes If you use a dial-up connection, placing a message in the Outbox folder doesn't actually send the message. You need to connect to the Internet and deliver the message to your mail server to send the message. If you use a high-speed connection and have Outlook Express set up to send messages immediately, the message is sent right after it arrives in the Outbox. You can tell Outlook Express that you don't want to send messages immediately by choosing the Tools menu's Options command and clearing the Send Messages Immediately check box.

Delivering E-Mail Messages

To deliver the messages in your Outbox folder to your outgoing mail server, click the Send And Receive toolbar button. (Depending on the display settings for your monitor, this toolbar button might be abbreviated Send/Recv.) If your computer isn't currently connected to the Internet, Windows establishes the connection. Then Windows delivers your outgoing messages and retrieves any incoming messages.

 Notes If you've already connected your computer to the Internet—perhaps you've been browsing the Web as described in Chapter 4—Outlook Express might automatically deliver your messages when you click the Send toolbar button on the Message window.

 Notes If you attempt to send and receive messages and receive an error saying that the connection to the mail server failed, wait and try to send and receive later. Your mail server or Internet connection might be down.

Creating and Using an Address Book

As soon as you start working with e-mail in Outlook Express, you'll want to begin building an Address Book, which you'll use to address the e-mail messages you send. Using the Address Book to store names and e-mail addresses makes the task of addressing the e-mail messages you create much quicker and reduces your chances of incorrectly addressing a message. You can add a name to your Address Book in two ways. To add a person's e-mail name and address to your Address Book if you've received a message from the person, follow these steps:

1   Double-click the message in the Folder Contents pane. Outlook Express opens a Message window for the message.

2   Right-click the From e-mail name and address information.

3   Choose the shortcut menu's Add To Address Book command, as shown in Figure 6-5.

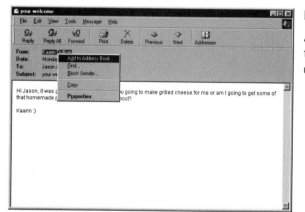

FIGURE 6-5

A Message window with the shortcut menu displayed.

6

4   This opens up a Properties dialog box, named after your user. When it opens, use the different tabs to enter additional information, and then press Enter or click OK.

To add a person's e-mail name and address to your Address Book if you haven't received a message from the person, follow these steps:

1   Click the Address Book toolbar button (depending on the size of your screen, this button's name might be abbreviated), or choose the Tools menu's Address Book command to display the Address Book, as shown in Figure 6-6.

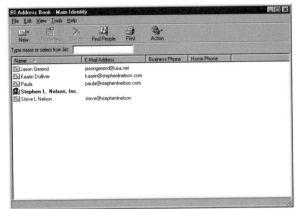

FIGURE 6-6

The Address Book window shows the e-mail names and addresses you've collected.

2   Click the New toolbar button, and then select New Contact from the drop-down menu to display the dialog box shown in Figure 6-7.

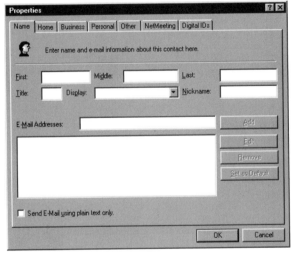

FIGURE 6-7

The Properties dialog box.

3   Enter the person's name in the Name boxes. Enter the person's full e-mail name and address in the E-Mail Addresses box.

4   Click Add. Outlook Express adds the e-mail name and address to your Address Book.

5   Click OK. Outlook Express displays the Address Book, which now shows the new name.

To use a name you've entered in the Address Book, follow these steps:

1 Click the New Mail toolbar button to display a New Message window.

2 Click the To address book icon to display the dialog box shown in Figure 6-8.

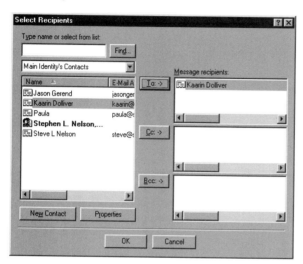

FIGURE 6-8

The Select Recipients dialog box shows the e-mail names and addresses you've collected.

 As long as a recipient's name is in the Address Book, you can enter it in the To box simply by typing the first few letters of the name. If Outlook Express recognizes the name, it completes the name for you.

3 To add a name to the To box, click the name to select it and then click To.

4 Click OK when you've finished collecting names from the Address Book. Then create your message in the usual way.

 If you're using the full version of Outlook instead of Outlook Express, you use the Contacts folder for storing contact information. To create a new contact, click Contacts on the Outlook bar and click the New toolbar button. Then use the window Outlook displays for entering the contact information.

Replying to E-Mail Messages

You can send a reply message to someone who's sent you a message. To reply to a message, follow these steps:

1 Select the message and click the Reply toolbar button, or choose the Message menu's Reply To Sender command. When you do this, Outlook Express creates a new message for you, filling in the To box with the e-mail name and address of the person to whom you're replying, as shown in Figure 6-9. Outlook Express also fills in the Subject box for you and then copies the original message text.

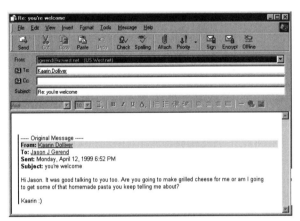

FIGURE 6-9

Reply to a message.

2 Add any new text to the message.

3 Delete any unneeded text from the original message text.

4 Click the Send toolbar button.

5 Click the Send And Receive toolbar button, and deliver the message in the usual way.

 To reply to a message and send a copy of your reply to every recipient of the original message, click the Reply All toolbar button or choose the Message menu's Reply To All command.

Forwarding E-Mail Messages

You can easily forward to someone else a copy of any message you receive. To forward a message, follow these steps:

1 Select the message and click the Forward toolbar button, or choose the Message menu's Forward command. When you do this, Outlook Express creates a new message for you, filling in the Subject box and then copying the original message text, as shown in Figure 6-10.

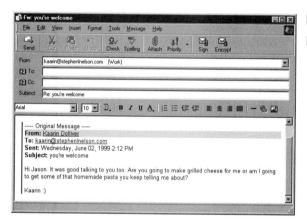

FIGURE 6-10

Forwarding a message.

2 Enter the message recipient's e-mail name and address in the To box.

3 Add any new text to the message.

4 Click the Send toolbar button.

5 Deliver the message in the usual way.

 The people to whom you send messages can also easily forward your messages to anyone else. For this reason, you probably shouldn't say anything in an e-mail message that you don't want repeated in public.

Deleting Messages

To delete a message in one of the Outlook Express folders, select it and then click the Delete toolbar button or press Delete. When you delete a message, Outlook Express moves the message to the Deleted Items folder. If you accidentally delete a message, you can still retrieve it. To retrieve a message, follow these steps:

1 Click the Deleted Items folder icon to open the folder. Its contents are displayed in the Folder Contents pane.

2 Select the messages you want to retrieve.

3 Drag and drop the messages in the folder in which you want to store the messages.

Because every message you delete actually gets moved to the Deleted Items folder, the number of messages stored in this folder grows quickly. To empty the Deleted Items folder, follow these steps:

1 Right-click the Deleted Items folder.

2 Choose the shortcut menu's Empty "Deleted Items" Folder command.

 After you delete a message from the Deleted Items folder or empty the Deleted Items folder, the message is permanently lost.

E-Mailing a File Attachment

Although most e-mail messages include only text, it's also possible to e-mail files. When you e-mail a file, you simply attach a copy of the file to the message. To e-mail a file **attachment**, follow these steps:

1 Click the New Mail toolbar button to display the New Mail window.

2 Enter the e-mail name of the message recipient in the To box.

3 Type a brief description of your message's subject in the Subject box.

4 Type your message in the large text box.

5 Click the Attach toolbar button, or choose the Insert menu's File Attachment command to display the Insert Attachment dialog box, as shown in Figure 6-11.

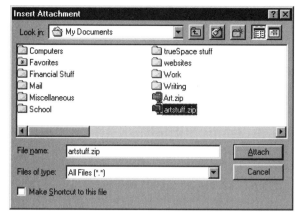

FIGURE 6-11

The Insert Attachment dialog box.

6 In the Look In drop-down list box, select the disk that contains the file you want. In the large list box, locate and double-click the folder that contains the file you want to attach.

7 Locate and double-click the file you want to attach to the message. Outlook Express attaches the file to the message, as shown in Figure 6-12.

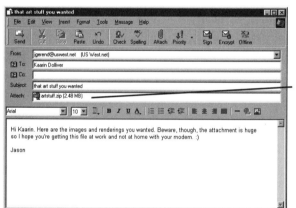

FIGURE 6-12

The Message window with message text and a file attachment.

The attachment.

 If you are e-mailing to or from an e-mail client other than Outlook Express or Netscape Messenger, you could have problems e-mailing files. Not all e-mail clients know how to read file attachments from other clients.

*If you send a message to someone and the message comes back to you, first verify that you entered the recipient's e-mail address correctly. If the message had an attachment, try sending a simple, plain text message without an attachment. If this works, verify the attachment size limits for the person's mail server. You might need to **zip** (compress) the attachment, send multiple attachments in individual messages, or separate a large archive of files into smaller archives and send them in multiple messages. If all else fails, call the recipient and tell him or her that you're having problems sending the message. If the recipient has had other people mention the same problem, he or she might be able to provide tips, an alternative e-mail address, or perhaps just assurance that the problem is on his or her side.*

If you receive a message with a file attachment, you can detach the file attachment from the message and permanently save it. To do this, follow these steps:

1 Double-click the message header in the Folder Contents pane to display the message in its own window.

2 Right-click the file in the Attach box.

3 Choose the shortcut menu's Save As command to display the Save As dialog box.

4 Name the file, and specify in which folder it should be saved. (If you don't specify a location, Outlook Express saves the attachment on your hard disk in the folder containing the last file you attached to a message in Outlook Express.)

 If you want to only open a file attachment—not save it—you can do so by double-clicking its icon.

 *Opening or saving e-mail file attachments is a common way to get a computer **virus**. Some viruses send a copy of themselves to everyone in an Address Book. So don't open or save a file attachment, even from a friend, unless the sender has told you the name of the file that he or she is sending to you.*

Using Netscape Messenger for E-Mail

This section describes how to use Netscape Messenger, the e-mail client that comes with Netscape Communicator. After reading this section you'll be able to accomplish the most important e-mailing tasks: reading e-mail messages, creating and delivering e-mail messages, building a list of e-mail **contacts**, replying to and forwarding e-mail messages, deleting e-mail messages, and attaching files to messages.

 Notes *Netscape Messenger version 4.51 is used throughout this section. If you have an older or newer version, features may look and work slightly differently from what is described here, but the overall feel will be very similar.*

Reading E-Mail Messages

To read your e-mail messages in Netscape Messenger, start the program. You can do this by clicking the Start button, choosing Programs, choosing Netscape Communicator, and then clicking Netscape Messenger. Alternately, you can start **Netscape Navigator** and then choose the Communicator menu's Messenger command. After you start Netscape Messenger, click the Inbox folder. Netscape Messenger lists your messages in the Folders pane and shows a message in the Message pane, as shown in Figure 6-13. To check for new messages, click the Get Msg toolbar button.

6

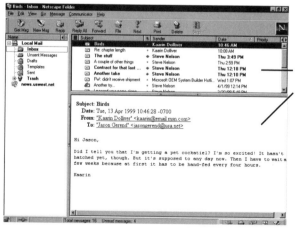

FIGURE 6-13

The Netscape Messenger program window.

This is the Folders pane.

This is the Message pane.

When you start Netscape Communicator or Messenger, Windows might display the Connect To dialog box so you can connect to the Internet. If this happens, click Connect if you want to retrieve new messages immediately. You can also choose to connect later, so you can read messages you've already downloaded or create new messages before connecting.

If you want to open a new window especially for a message—perhaps so you can see more of the message—double-click the message in the Folder Contents pane. Netscape Messenger opens a window for the message. After you read the message, click the Close button.

Creating and Delivering E-Mail Messages

To create an e-mail message using Netscape Messenger, follow these steps:

1 Click the New Msg toolbar button to display the Composition window, as shown in Figure 6-14.

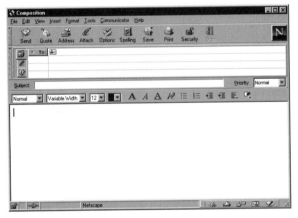

FIGURE 6-14

A blank Composition window.

2 Enter the message recipient's e-mail name in the To box.

You can send a message or message copy to more than one recipient. To do this, enter e-mail names separated by semicolons.

3 Type a brief description of your message's subject in the Subject box.

4 Type your message in the large text box. Figure 6-15 shows a partial message.

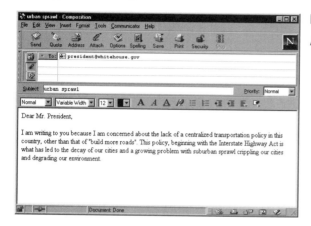

FIGURE 6-15

A partial message.

5 Optionally, use the Message window's Formatting toolbar buttons to format your message.

 *In order to properly view a message with formatting in it, the recipient of your message must use an e-mail client program (like Netscape Messenger or Outlook Express) that understands how to display the formatting you apply. If you send a message with formatting to a person listed in your **Address Book** as unable to view **HTML** (formatted) messages, Netscape Messenger will ask whether you want to send it formatted as Plain Text, HTML, or both.*

 To check the spelling in your message, click the Spelling toolbar button. If Netscape Messenger finds an incorrectly spelled word, it displays a dialog box in which you can correct the misspelling.

6 After you finish typing your message, click the Send toolbar button to deliver it. After you click Send, Windows might display the Connect To dialog box to ask whether it should connect you to the Internet so you can send the message. If you want to connect and deliver the message immediately, click Connect. If you choose not to connect and deliver the message, it is placed in the Unsent Messages folder and is delivered the next time you connect and click the Get Msg toolbar button.

 Notes *If you attempt to send and receive messages and receive an error saying that the connection to the mail server failed, wait and try to send and receive later. Your mail server or Internet connection might be down.*

Creating and Using an Address Book

As soon as you start working with e-mail in Netscape Messenger, you'll want to begin building an Address Book, which you'll use to address your e-mail messages. Using the Address Book to store names and e-mail addresses makes the task of addressing the e-mail messages you create much quicker and reduces your chances of incorrectly addressing a message. You can add a name to your Address Book in two ways. To add a person's e-mail name and address to your Address Book if you've received a message from the person, follow these steps:

1 Double-click the message in the Folder Contents pane. Netscape Messenger opens a Message window for the message.

2 Click the name of the person who sent you the message to add that person's information to your Address Book.

3 In the New Card dialog box, shown in Figure 6-16, use the different tabs to enter additional information, and then click OK.

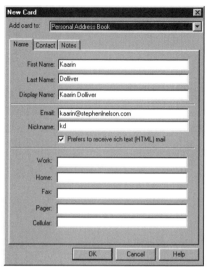

FIGURE 6-16

The New Card dialog box appears when you add a name to your Address Book.

To add a person's e-mail name and address to your Address Book if you haven't received a message from the person, follow these steps:

1 Choose the Communicator menu's Address Book command to display the Address Book window, as shown in Figure 6-17.

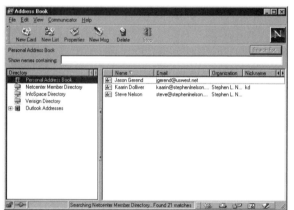

FIGURE 6-17

The Address Book window shows the e-mail names and addresses you've collected.

2 Click the New Card toolbar button to display the dialog box shown in Figure 6-18.

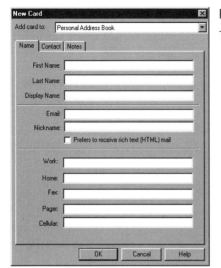

FIGURE 6-18

The New Card dialog box.

3 Enter the person's name in the Name boxes—First and Last. Enter the person's full e-mail address in the Email box.

4 Optionally, enter a nickname for the person, and specify whether the person can receive HTML-formatted messages.

5 Click OK. Netscape Messenger displays the Address Book dialog box, which now shows the new name.

To use a name you've entered in the Address Book, follow these steps:

1 Click the New Msg toolbar button to display the Composition window.

2 Click the Address toolbar button to display the dialog box shown in Figure 6-19.

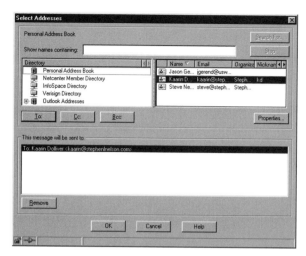

FIGURE 6-19

The Select Addresses
dialog box shows the
e-mail addresses you've
collected and also lets you
search for a person's
address on the Internet.

 As long as a recipient's name is in the Address Book, you can enter it in the To box simply by typing the first few letters of the name. If Netscape Messenger recognizes the name, it completes the name for you.

3   To add a name to the To box, click the name to select it and then click To.

4   Click OK when you've finished collecting names from the Address Book. Then create your message in the usual way.

Replying to E-Mail Messages

You can send a reply message to someone who's sent you a message. To reply to a message, follow these steps:

1   Select the message, and click the Reply toolbar button. When you do this, Netscape Messenger creates a new message for you, filling in the To box with the e-mail name and address of the person to whom you're replying. Netscape Messenger also fills in the Subject box for you and then copies the original message text, as shown in Figure 6-20.

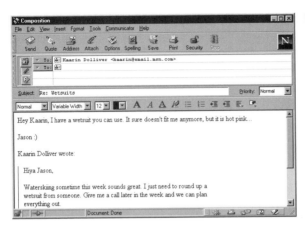

FIGURE 6-20

Reply to a message.

2 Add any new text to the message.

3 Delete any unneeded text from the original message text.

4 Click the Send toolbar button.

To reply to a message and send a copy of your reply to every recipient of the original message, click the Reply All toolbar button or choose the Message menu's Reply To All command.

Forwarding E-Mail Messages

You can easily forward a copy of any message you receive to someone else. To forward a message, follow these steps:

1 Select the message and click the Forward toolbar button, or choose the Message menu's Forward command. When you do this, Netscape Messenger creates a new message for you, filling in the Subject box and then copying the original message text.

2 Enter the message recipient's e-mail name and address in the To box.

3 Add any new text to the message.

4 Click the Send toolbar button.

5 Deliver the message in the usual way.

The people to whom you send messages can also easily forward your messages to anyone else. For this reason, you probably shouldn't say anything in an e-mail message that you don't want repeated in public.

Deleting Messages

To delete a message in one of the Netscape Messenger folders, select it and then click the Delete toolbar button or press Delete. You can also right-click the message and choose the shortcut menu's Delete command.

When you delete a message, Netscape Messenger moves the message to the Trash folder. If you accidentally delete a message, you can still retrieve it. To retrieve a message, follow these steps:

1   Click the Deleted Items folder icon to open the folder. Its contents are displayed in the Folder Contents pane.

2   Select the message you want to retrieve.

3   Drag the message to the folder listed in the Folders pane in which you want to store the message.

 Because every message you delete actually gets moved to the Trash folder, the number of messages stored in this folder grows quickly. To empty the Trash folder, choose the File menu's Empty Trash On Local Mail command.

 After you empty the Trash folder, all deleted messages are permanently lost.

E-Mailing a File Attachment

Although most e-mail messages include only text, it's also possible to e-mail files. When you e-mail a file, you simply attach a copy of the file to the message. To e-mail a file **attachment**, follow these steps:

1   Click the New Msg toolbar button to display the New Mail window.

2   Enter the e-mail name of the message recipient in the To box.

3   In the Subject box, type a brief description of your message's subject.

4   Type your message in the large text box.

5   Click the Attach toolbar button, and then choose File from the drop-down menu to display the dialog box shown in Figure 6-21.

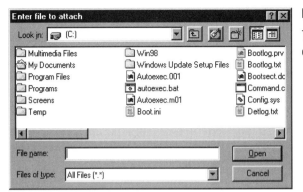

FIGURE 6-21

The Enter File To Attach
dialog box.

6   In the Look In drop-down list box, select the disk that contains
    the file you want. In the large list box, locate and double-click the
    folder that contains the file you want to attach.

7   Locate and double-click the file you want to attach to the mes-
    sage. Netscape Messenger attaches the file to the message, as
    shown in Figure 6-22.

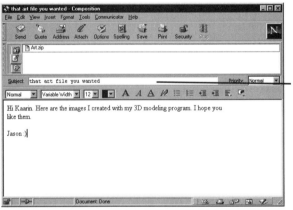

FIGURE 6-22

The Composition window
with message text and a
file attachment.

— The attachment.

  To delete a file that you attached to a message before you send the
message, click the file and then press Delete.

*If you send a message to someone and the message comes back to you, first verify that you entered the recipient's e-mail address correctly. If the message had an attachment, try sending a simple, plain text message without an attachment. If this works, verify the attachment size limits for the person's mail server. You might need to **zip** (compress) the attachment, send multiple attachments in individual messages, or separate a large archive of files into smaller archives and send them in multiple messages. If all else fails, call the recipient and tell him or her that you're having problems sending the message. If the recipient has had other people mention the same problem, he or she might be able to provide tips, an alternative e-mail address, or perhaps just assurance that the problem is on his or her side.*

If you receive a message with a file attachment, you can detach the file attachment from the message and permanently save it. To do this, follow these steps:

1 Double-click the message header in the Folder Contents pane to display the message in its own window.

2 Click the **hyperlink** to the file at the bottom of the message window.

3 Click the Save It To Disk option button, and then press Enter to display the Save As dialog box.

4 Name the file, and specify in which folder it should be saved. (If you don't specify a location, Netscape Messenger saves the attachment on your hard disk in the folder containing the last file you attached to a message in Netscape Messenger.)

*Opening or saving e-mail file attachments is a common way to get a computer **virus**. Some viruses send a copy of themselves to everyone in an Address Book. So don't open or save a file attachment, even from a friend, unless the sender has told you the name of the file that he or she is sending to you.*

CHAPTER 7

Working with Newsgroups

Newsgroups are another way to share information over the **Internet.** Working with newsgroups and newsgroup messages is very similar to working with **e-mail** and e-mail messages, as described in the previous chapter. The major difference is that instead of sending a message directly to a specific person or group of people, you post it to a location that typically holds many messages with the same topic in common. Then other people who have access to this location can visit it and browse the messages posted there. This chapter describes how to work with **Microsoft Outlook Express** and **Netscape Messenger,** the two most popular programs used for reading and posting newsgroup messages, by covering the following newsgroup topics:

- What newsgroups are and how they work
- Using Deja.com to search newsgroups
- Using Outlook Express with newsgroups
- Using Netscape Messenger

 Notes | *Chapter 2 describes how to set up an Internet connection. Chapter 6 describes how to use Outlook Express and Netscape Messenger to work with e-mail.*

What Newsgroups Are and How They Work

A newsgroup works like a bulletin board where people post messages for other people to read. Typically, you use a newsreader to post and read the messages posted to a newsgroup. Because there are perhaps hundreds of thousands of people who post messages on thousands of different topics and millions of people who want to read these messages, each newsgroup contains only those messages that fall into a specific category. For example, there's a newsgroup for fans of *Star Wars,* a newsgroup for people who enjoy mountain climbing, and a newsgroup devoted to topics on photography. And as you might expect, there are hundreds and hundreds of newsgroups for specialty computer topics.

Using Deja.com to Search Newsgroups

One of the main problems with newsgroups is that it can be difficult to find what you're looking for. Newsreaders typically have only limited search capabilities, so to find topics on newsgroups it's often best to perform a search using Deja.com. The Deja.com **web site** provides an index-style **search engine** for **Usenet** newsgroups. It also provides a directory of newsgroups organized into categories, which can be useful in locating newsgroups about topics of interest to you.

 Notes   *Usenet is a worldwide network, mainly of UNIX machines, that hosts tens of thousands of newsgroups.*

Searching with Deja.com

To use Deja.com to search for a particular topic, follow these steps:

1 Start your **web browser**, and connect to the Internet if you aren't currently connected.

2 Enter *http://www.deja.com* in the Address or Location box on your browser. This takes you to the Deja.com web site, shown in Figure 7-1.

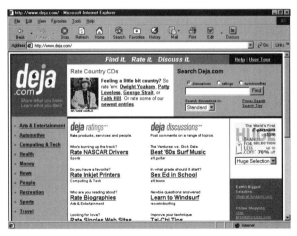

FIGURE 7-1

Deja.com is a search engine for newsgroups.

3 Enter the text you want to search for in the Find text box in the upper right of the page.

4 Optionally, search for a message, a newsgroup, or a Deja.com community by clicking the Discussions, Ratings, or Communities option buttons.

5 Optionally, select the type of entries you want to find from the Search Discussion In drop-down list box, such as Standard, Jobs, or For Sale.

6 Click Find.

7 Deja.com displays the search results with the closest matches listed first (see Figure 7-2). To view a message, click the **hyperlinked** subject.

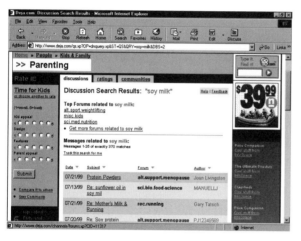

FIGURE 7-2

Deja.com displays a list of messages or newsgroups that match your keywords.

 You can sort the results by Date, Score, Subject, Forum (Newsgroup), or Author by clicking a sort field.

Using the Deja.com Directory

To use Deja.com to browse newsgroups by category, follow these steps:

1 Click one of the broad categories on the left side of the **web page.**

2 To browse a subcategory, click one of the subcategories at the top of the page displayed, or scroll down the page to see more information about the current category.

3 When you find the newsgroup you want to view, click the newsgroup to view its current messages (see Figure 7-3).

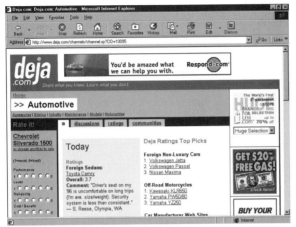

FIGURE 7-3

Deja.com also maintains a useful listing of newsgroups by category.

Performing Advanced Searches

To perform a more powerful search of newsgroups using Deja.com, follow these steps:

1 Click the Power Search hyperlink to display the Power Search web page, as shown in Figure 7-4.

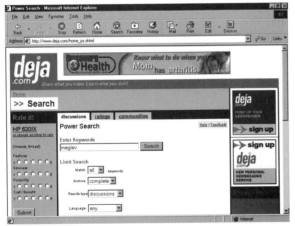

FIGURE 7-4

Use the Power Search page to gain more control over your newsgroup searches.

2 Enter your search keywords in the Enter Keywords box.

3 In the Match drop-down list box under Limit Search, select All to return only messages that match all your keywords, or select Any to display messages that match any of your keywords.

4 In the Language drop-down list box, specify the language you want for the messages.

5 If you want to search for keywords in the subject field of a message, enter the keyword in the Subject box.

6 To search a specific newsgroup only, enter the newsgroup name in the Forum box.

7 Enter an author name in the Author box.

8 Enter a date for the oldest message in the Date From box, and then enter a date for the newest message in the To box.

9 In the Sort By drop-down list box under Organize Results, specify a format for your results.

10 In the Results Per Page drop-down list box, specify the number of results you want displayed on a page.

11 Click Search to search the newsgroups for messages that match your criteria (see Figure 7-5).

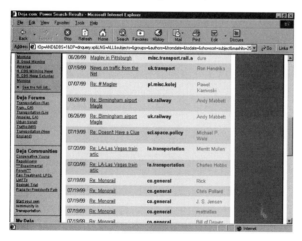

FIGURE 7-5

These results are organized by thread.

Using Outlook Express with Newsgroups

This section describes how to use Outlook Express to accomplish the most common newsgroup tasks: finding newsgroups, subscribing to newsgroups, reading newsgroup messages, posting messages to newsgroups, and working offline with newsgroups.

You aren't limited to using Outlook Express to benefit from this section, however, because the basic concepts apply to other newsreaders. If you use Netscape Messenger as your newsreader, see the next section, "Using Netscape Messenger with Newsgroups," for information on using Netscape Messenger with newsgroups.

Notes *Outlook Express version 5 is used throughout this section. If you have an older or newer version, features may look and work slightly differently from those described here, but the overall feel will be very similar.*

Setting Up a News Account

Before you can view newsgroups, you need to set up Outlook Express to work with your news **server.** If you use a large **ISP** for your Internet connection, you may have already set up Outlook Express when you installed your Internet software. Otherwise, to set up your news server, follow these steps:

1 Start Outlook Express by either clicking its icon on the Quick Launch toolbar next to the Start button or by clicking the Start button, choosing Programs, and then clicking Outlook Express.

2 Choose the Tools menu's Account command, and then click the News tab in the dialog box shown in Figure 7-6.

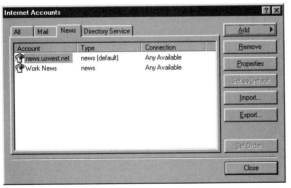

FIGURE 7-6

Use the Internet Accounts dialog box to view and change all your news- and mail-related account settings.

3 If no news servers are set up, click Add and then click News.

4 In the Display Name box, enter the name you want to appear on your messages, and then click Next.

5 Enter your e-mail address in the E-Mail Address box, and then click Next.

6 In the News Server box, enter the news server (NNTP server) provided to you by your ISP, as shown in Figure 7-7.

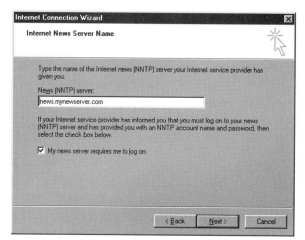

FIGURE 7-7

Enter the news server address provided to you by your ISP.

7 Select the My News Server Requires Me To Log On check box if your news server uses authentication (contact your ISP if you're unsure about any of these settings), and then click Next.

8 If your news server requires you to log in, enter your user name and **password** in the next window, or select Log On Using Secure Password Authentication if your server requires it, and then click Next.

9 Click Finish.

Subscribing to a Newsgroup

After you subscribe to a newsgroup, you can then easily visit the newsgroup and read or post messages. To subscribe to a newsgroup—which doesn't cost anything, by the way—follow these steps:

1 Start Outlook Express by either clicking its icon on the Quick Launch toolbar next to the Start button or by clicking the Start button, choosing Programs, and then clicking Outlook Express.

2 Connect to the Internet if you aren't currently connected.

3 Select your news server in the Folder pane.

4 Click the Newsgroups toolbar button. Outlook Express lists under the All tab all the newsgroups that your ISP carries on that news server (see Figure 7-8). The Subscribed tab shows a list of newsgroups to which you're currently subscribed, and the New tab shows newsgroups that were added since you last viewed the list of newsgroups.

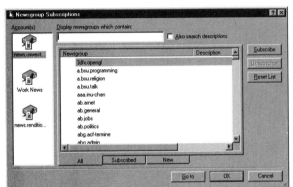

FIGURE 7-8

Outlook Express lists the newsgroups available on the news server.

 The first time you view the list of newsgroups, Outlook Express downloads the list from your news server, which can take quite a while.

---

5 Scroll through the list of newsgroups. When you find one to which you want to subscribe, double-click it. You can subscribe to as many newsgroups as you want.

6 Select a newsgroup, and click Go To if you want to view the newsgroup immediately. Otherwise, click OK when you're finished.

To find newsgroups that cover a topic you're interested in, enter a topic name in the Display Newsgroups Which Contain box. A list of newsgroups with the topic name appears. You can also select the Also Search Descriptions check box to search the descriptions of newsgroups—when available.

To unsubscribe from a newsgroup, select the newsgroup in the Folders pane, press Delete, and then click OK.

Reading Newsgroup Messages

After you've subscribed to a newsgroup, you can then read the messages that people have posted. To read a newsgroup's messages, follow these steps:

1 Click the newsgroup name in the Folders pane. If the news server branch of the list isn't expanded, you might need to do this by clicking the plus sign (+) to the left of the news server name. Outlook Express then retrieves a list of the newsgroup messages from the news server, as shown in Figure 7-9.

2 Click the message header (the subject) that you want to read in the Folder Contents pane. Outlook Express displays the message in the Preview pane. If you want to open a window for a message, double-click the message.

3 To view messages in a **conversation**, click the plus sign next to the message to see a list of messages about the same topic.

 A conversation is a list of messages on the same subject that are grouped together.

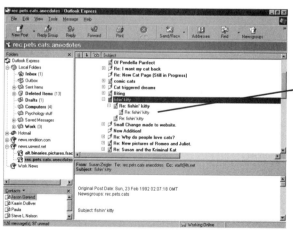

FIGURE 7-9

To read a newsgroup message, click or double-click the message header.

This is a conversation.

4 To "watch" a conversation for new messages, click the blank space next to the plus sign for the conversation you want to watch. When the conversation has new messages, you'll see the message change colors.

5 To **download** additional message headers in the newsgroup, choose the Tools menu's Get Next 300 Headers command.

---

 *Some newsgroup messages include file **attachments**. To save a file attachment that's part of a newsgroup message, right-click the attachment and then choose the shortcut menu's Save As command.*

 Sometimes you'll find a file posted on a newsgroup in the form of multiple messages that need to be put together to properly open the file. To put together multiple messages into a single file, select all the messages that make up the file, choose the File menu's Combine And Decode command, use the Move Up and Move Down buttons to arrange the files in proper order, and then click OK.

Posting a Newsgroup Message

To post a message to a newsgroup, click the newsgroup name in the Folders list and then click the New Post toolbar button. When Outlook Express displays a New Message window, enter a brief description in the Subject box and then enter your message, as shown in Figure 7-10.

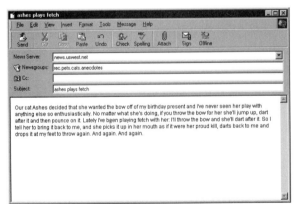

FIGURE 7-10

A partially completed newsgroup post.

When you're finished, click the Send toolbar button to post your message to the newsgroup.

Even though it's easy to quickly get on a newsgroup and start posting messages, it's usually a good idea to "lurk" a little bit first (i.e., observe what goes on in the newsgroup). Also, if you have a question that you want answered, search Deja.com before you ask it—chances are it's already been answered for somebody else.

 *If you post messages to newsgroups, you tend to receive lots of unsolicited e-mail (called **spam**) from people who want to sell you various products and services—including many products or services that you might find offensive. Some people add the prefix "nospam" to their e-mail address to prevent this from happening, but your success with this method may vary.*

Setting Up Newsgroups for Offline Viewing

One of the drawbacks of newsgroups is that downloading all the message headers can take a significant amount of time. Then after you find a message you want to open, you have to wait again while the message body downloads. If you have a slow dial-up connection or need to minimize the amount of time you spend connected to the Internet, you can configure your newsreader to download messages all at once and then disconnect, so you can read the messages offline (while disconnected). This technique is known as synchronizing. To set up the newsgroups that you want Outlook Express to download, follow these steps:

1 Select your news server (not a newsgroup) from the Folders pane.

2 Outlook Express displays in the pane on the right a list of newsgroups to which you subscribe (see Figure 7-11), along with their current synchronization settings. If you want Outlook Express to download new messages in the newsgroup, select the check box next to New Messages Only for the newsgroup you want Outlook Express to **synchronize**.

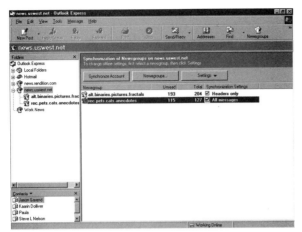

FIGURE 7-11

Configuring Outlook
Express to download your
newsgroups so you can
read them offline.

3 To change the synchronization settings for a newsgroup, select a newsgroup, and then click Settings. To turn off any synchronization for the newsgroup, choose Don't Synchronize from the drop-down menu. To download all the messages in the newsgroup, choose All Messages. To download only the new headers (subject names) in the newsgroup, choose Headers Only.

4 Click Synchronize Account to connect to the Internet and synchronize the newsgroups you set up for offline viewing.

 If you're viewing a newsgroup with lots of images or other files attached to the messages, you may want to choose the Headers Only setting to save time when downloading the newsgroup. You can then browse the headers and mark only the individual messages you want to download.

Working with Newsgroups Offline

After you download a list of headers for the newsgroup you want to view by either opening the newsgroup while connected to the Internet or by synchronizing the newsgroup, you can disconnect from the Internet and work with your newsgroups offline. To do this, follow these steps:

1 Open the newsgroup you want to view.

2 Choose the File menu's Work Offline command to work offline.

3 Click a downloaded message to read it (see Figure 7-12).

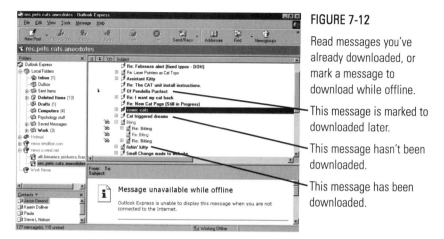

FIGURE 7-12

Read messages you've already downloaded, or mark a message to download while offline.

This message is marked to downloaded later.

This message hasn't been downloaded.

This message has been downloaded.

4   Mark any message you want to download the next time you synchronize the newsgroup by right-clicking the message and choosing the shortcut menu's Download Message Later command.

5   When you're ready to synchronize the newsgroup you're viewing, choose the Tools menu's Synchronize Newsgroup command. Optionally, modify the synchronization options in the Synchronize Newsgroup dialog box, and then click OK.

Using Netscape Messenger with Newsgroups

This section describes how to use Netscape Messenger, the e-mail and news **client** that comes with **Netscape Communicator,** to accomplish the most common newsgroup tasks: subscribing to newsgroups, reading newsgroup messages, posting messages to newsgroups, and working offline with newsgroups. The procedures outlined in this section apply to Netscape Messenger as well as to other newsreaders.

Notes   *Netscape Messenger version 4.51 is used throughout this section. If you have an older or newer version, features may look and work slightly differently from what is described here, but the overall feel will be very similar.*

Subscribing to a Newsgroup

By subscribing to a newsgroup, you can then easily visit the newsgroup and read or post messages. To subscribe to a newsgroup—which you can do for free, by the way—follow these steps:

1 To start Netscape Messenger, click the Start button, choose Programs, choose Netscape Communicator, and then click Netscape Messenger. Alternately, start **Netscape Navigator** and then choose the Communicator menu's Messenger command.

2 Connect to the Internet if you aren't currently connected.

3 Right-click your news **server** in the Folders pane, and choose the shortcut menu's Subscribe To Newsgroups command to display the dialog box shown in Figure 7-13.

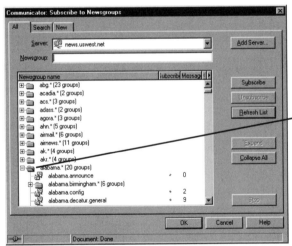

FIGURE 7-13

The Subscribe To Newsgroups dialog box lists the newsgroups available on the news server.

Click a folder to display the newsgroups about the general topic.

4 Scroll through the list of newsgroups. Folders are general topics that contain newsgroups inside them. Click a folder to view the newsgroups about a topic.

In the Newsgroup box, type the first few letters of the newsgroup you want to go to in order to jump quickly to that part of the newsgroup list.

5 When you find a newsgroup to which you want to subscribe, double-click it. You can subscribe to as many newsgroups as you want.

6 To search for a particular newsgroup, click the Search tab, enter your search text in the Search For box, and then click Search Now. Netscape Messenger lists the newsgroups with names that contain the text you entered (see Figure 7-14).

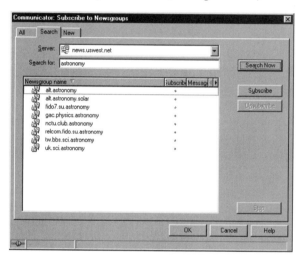

FIGURE 7-14

Use the Search tab to perform a quick search for a newsgroup.

 When you search for a newsgroup, Netscape Messenger lists only newsgroups with names containing the exact text you enter.

7 To view a list of newsgroups that were created since you last downloaded the list of newsgroups, click the New tab.

8 Click OK when you're finished subscribing to newsgroups.

 To unsubscribe from a newsgroup, select the newsgroup in the Folders pane, press Delete, and then click OK.

Reading Newsgroup Messages

After you've subscribed to a newsgroup, you can then read the messages people have posted. To read a newsgroup's messages, follow these steps:

1 Click the newsgroup name in the Folders pane. If the news server branch of the list isn't expanded, you might need to expand it by clicking the plus sign (+) to the left of the news server name. Netscape Messenger then retrieves a list of the newsgroup messages from the news server (see Figure 7-15).

2 In the Folder Contents pane, click the message header that you want to read. Netscape Messenger displays the message in the Preview pane. If you want to open a window for a message, double-click the message.

3 To view messages in a **conversation**, click the plus sign next to the message to see a list of messages about the same topic.

Notes   *A conversation is a list of messages on the same subject that are grouped together.*

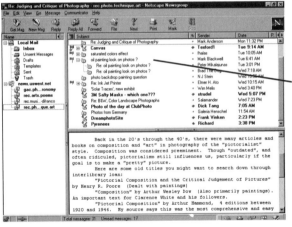

FIGURE 7-15

To read a newsgroup message, click or double-click the message header.

This is a conversation.

4 To "watch" a conversation for new messages, right-click the conversation you want to watch and choose the shortcut menu's Watch Thread command. When the conversation has new messages, you'll see the message change colors.

5 To download additional headers in the newsgroup, choose the File menu's Get Next 500 Messages command.

Posting a Newsgroup Message

To post a message to a newsgroup, click the newsgroup name in the Folders list and then click the New Msg toolbar button. When Netscape Messenger displays a new Composition window, enter a subject description in the box provided and then enter your message (see Figure 7-16). The steps for creating a newsgroup message closely resemble the steps for creating a regular e-mail message.

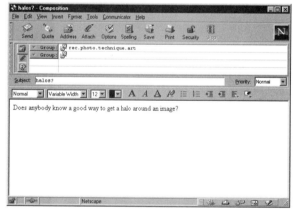

FIGURE 7-16

A partially completed newsgroup post.

When you're finished, click the Send toolbar button to post your message to the newsgroup.

*If you post messages to newsgroups, you tend to receive lots of unsolicited e-mail (called **spam**) from people who want to sell you various products and services—including many that you might find offensive. Some people add the prefix "nospam" to their e-mail address to prevent this from happening, but the results may be less than perfect.*

Setting Up Newsgroups for Offline Viewing

One of the drawbacks with newsgroups is that downloading all the message headers can take a significant amount of time. Then when you want to open a message, you have to wait some more while the message body is downloaded. If you have a slow dial-up connection or need to minimize the amount of time you spend connected to the Internet, you can configure your newsreader to download messages all at once and then disconnect, so that you can read the messages offline (while disconnected). This is a technique known as **synchronizing.** To set up the newsgroups you want Netscape Messenger to download, follow these steps:

1 Choose the File menu's Offline command, and then choose Synchronize from the submenu to display the dialog box shown in Figure 7-17.

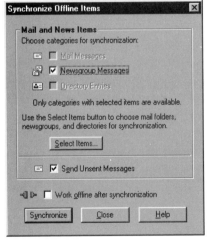

FIGURE 7-17

Use the Synchronize Offline Items dialog box to download any newsgroups you want to read while disconnected from the Internet.

2 Click Select Items to display the dialog box shown in Figure 7-18.

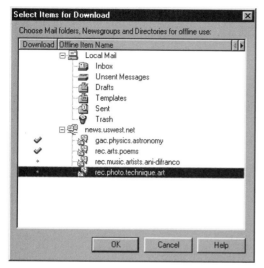

FIGURE 7-18

Use the Select Items For Download dialog box to select the newsgroups you want to download.

3 Click the dot next to the groups you want to download to place a check mark in the Download column.

4 Click OK, and then click Synchronize if you want to download the newsgroups right away. Otherwise, click Close.

5 To disconnect from the Internet and work offline, choose the File menu's Offline command and then choose Work Offline from the submenu.

If you want to download a few specific messages, select the messages, choose the Message menu's Mark command, and then choose Flag from the submenu. To download the flagged messages, choose the File menu's Offline command and then choose Get Flagged Messages from the submenu.

7

CHAPTER 8

Chatting Online

Chatting on the **Internet** is one of the most popular—and habit-forming—ways to spend your time online. People from all over the world gather in various types of **chat rooms** to discuss just about every topic you can imagine (and perhaps some you don't want to imagine). This chapter describes the following topics related to Internet chatting:

- Different ways to chat
- Using **Microsoft Chat** for **IRC**
- Using mIRC for IRC
- Using ICQ
- Using Yahoo! Chat
- Using **AOL Instant Messenger**

 Notes *Many people use chat services to look for love, and some are less than discreet about it. If you don't like the way a conversation progresses in a chat room, just exit the room or switch chat **servers**.*

Different Ways to Chat

Chatting on the Internet used to consist solely of text-only messages, but as the popularity of this pastime grew, so did the different methods used for chatting. You can now use the current standard for text chat, known as Internet Relay Chat. You can also use chat programs that allow you to use cartoon characters to represent your image. Alternately, on the World Wide Web, you can send instant messages via a pagerlike piece of software, or you can even chat in 3-D worlds or via audio and video teleconferencing. This section describes the main methods available for chatting online.

IRC is currently the most popular form of **online** chatting. IRC is a system in which you send real-time text messages to other people over the Internet. The latest IRC programs can also transmit files and sounds and, in the case of Microsoft Chat, use cartoon characters to represent emotions. In order to use IRC to talk with other users, you need an IRC **client**, such as mIRC (discussed later in the section "Using mIRC for IRC") or Microsoft Chat (discussed later in the section "Using Microsoft Chat for IRC"), as shown in Figure 8-1.

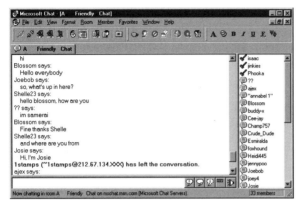

FIGURE 8-1

Microsoft Chat is an IRC client.

Because IRC programs were somewhat difficult to set up and use, Web-based chat rooms developed. Chat rooms on **web pages** are essentially Web-based versions of IRC, in which you exchange real-time text messages by using a **web browser** instead of an IRC program. The convenience of Web-based chatting has also allowed **web sites** to host their own chat rooms, such as Yahoo! Chat (discussed later in the section "Using Yahoo! Chat").

FIGURE 8-2

Yahoo! Chat is a Web-based chat system.

Another type of chat program that has grown tremendously in popularity is the instant messenger, with ICQ ("I Seek You") and America Online (AOL) Instant Messenger currently the market leaders. Instant messengers are small programs that you leave running while you're on the Internet. The program allows you to send messages to friends and associates who are also online, who can in turn contact you instantly and send you messages while you're online, sort of like an Internet pager. This type of chat program is designed to make it easier to chat with people you already know, unlike other types of chat programs in which the emphasis is more on meeting new people. For more information on instant messengers, see the section "Using ICQ."

One form of chatting that is gaining favor is the three-dimensional (3-D) virtual world that allows you to create buildings and landscapes and then chat with other people in these settings through the use of avatars. An avatar, which is a computer-generated model that can be anything from a camera-toting tourist to a giant guppy, represents you in the virtual world. As your avatar navigates the world, you chat with other people by typing messages to them. You can add simple animation by instructing your avatar to wave, smile, or even do the Macarena. These 3-D worlds are the future of the Internet, but they still have a way to go before they supplant normal chat methods and standard web pages. Objects in the worlds frequently take too long to **download**, graphics are often primitive and slow, and the worlds can be empty and uninspired. Still, many users of these systems refuse to go back to standard chat rooms after tasting the future of the Web. In order to use these 3-D worlds, you may need a special program (such as Active Worlds' proprietary browser, shown in Figure 8-3) or a Virtual Reality Modeling Language (VRML) plug-in for your web browser. (Both **Netscape Communicator** and Microsoft Internet Explorer allow for a VRML plug-in as an option during installation.)

8

FIGURE 8-3

Active Worlds is a 3-D chat program.

Another way to chat that is developing along with the rise of faster connection speeds is audio and video teleconferencing. Programs such as **Microsoft NetMeeting** and CUSeeMe let users have one-on-one text, voice, video, and whiteboard chat sessions. However, these programs can be difficult to configure and require a fast Internet connection to work well. The current level of audio quality is low, and video is jerky and grainy. These conditions will gradually improve as faster Internet connection methods such as **DSL** and cable modems grow in popularity, but until then, audio and video teleconferencing will remain somewhat limited in appeal for most users.

Using Microsoft Chat for IRC

Microsoft Chat is an easy-to-use IRC client that comes free with Internet Explorer. In addition to being easy to use, it also has the unique feature of allowing you to use a cartoon character to represent yourself online, making Microsoft Chat a little more visually appealing and fun.

 If you can't find Microsoft Chat, you probably don't have it installed. To install Microsoft Chat, click the Start button, choose Settings, and click Control Panel. Double-click the Add/Remove Programs icon, select Microsoft Internet Explorer and Internet Tools, and then click Add/Remove. Click the Add A Component option button, click OK, and then use the **wizard** provided to download and install Microsoft Chat. The option to install Microsoft Chat is located in the Communications Components category.

Starting Microsoft Chat and Joining a Chat Room

To use Microsoft Chat, follow these steps:

1 Click the Start button, choose Programs, choose Accessories, choose Internet Tools, and then click Microsoft Chat. The first time you start Microsoft Chat, you select a chat server and enter your user information in the dialog box that displays (see Figure 8-4).

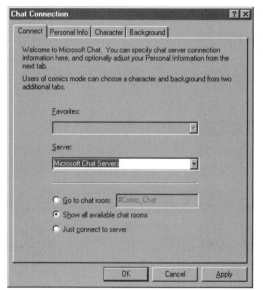

FIGURE 8-4

Use the Chat Connection dialog box to connect to a chat server.

2 Select a chat server from the Server drop-down list box.

 If you want to use the Comic characters in Microsoft Chat, select Microsoft Chat Servers from the Server drop-down list box.

3 If you know the chat room you want to go to, click the Go To Chat Room option button and type the chat room name in the text box.

4 If you want to see a list of chat rooms when you connect, click the Show All Available Chat Rooms option button.

5 Next, click the Personal Info tab, shown in Figure 8-5, to enter information about yourself that you want other chat users to see.

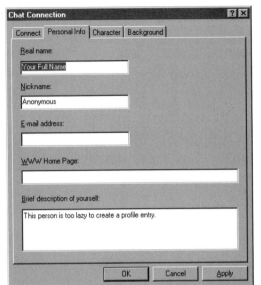

FIGURE 8-5

Use the Personal Info tab to enter information about yourself.

6 Click the Character tab to select a character to represent yourself to other Microsoft Chat users (see Figure 8-6).

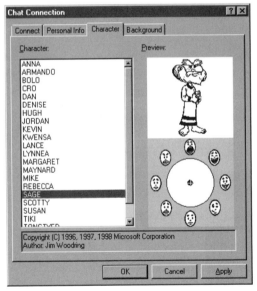

FIGURE 8-6

Use the Character tab to select a character to represent yourself while you chat.

7 Click OK when you're finished to connect to the chat server. If you chose to see a list of chat rooms in step 4, the Chat Room List dialog box opens, as shown in Figure 8-7.

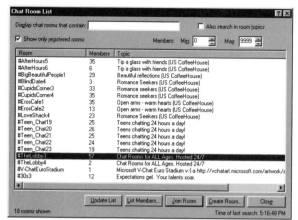

FIGURE 8-7

Use the Chat Room List to select the chat room you want to visit.

 Clear the Show Only Registered Rooms check box to a see a complete list of chat rooms (including many unconventional rooms).

---

8 Select a room from the list, and then click Join Room to begin chatting.

 To create your own chat room, click Create Room and use the Create Chat Room dialog box to set up your chat room.

Chatting in Comics View and Text View

If you connected to Microsoft Chat Servers, you'll probably want to use the Comics view to chat. Because most people on Microsoft Chat Servers are also using Microsoft Chat, they use the Comics view to communicate emotions and expressions, thus adding variety and making communication a little easier—that is, if you're also in Comics view. If you're on a different chat server, you should probably stick to the Text view unless you've visited the room before and know what the other characters in the room will look like.

To use the Comics view and Text view to chat, follow these steps:

1 Enter a chat room.

You can use the Comics view in any chat room, although the characters assigned to other users will be assigned at random unless they are also using Microsoft Chat. In most cases, you should stick to Text view when venturing off the Microsoft servers.

2 To turn on Comics view, click the Comics View toolbar button to display the room in Comics view, as shown in Figure 8-8.

FIGURE 8-8

Type your text in the text box at the lower left, and use the circle on the right to change the expression of your character.

3 Click the facial expression of your choice.

4 Click in the circle surrounded by facial expressions in the bottom right of your screen to change the expression of your character.

5 If you want to switch to Text view, click View and then click Plain Text. This displays the room in Text view, as shown in Figure 8-9.

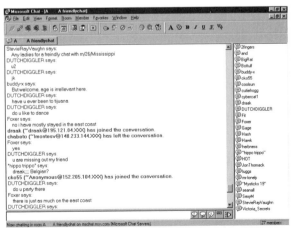

FIGURE 8-9

Click the Text View toolbar button to use Microsoft Chat as a text-only IRC client.

6 To say something in the room, enter text in the text box at the bottom of the screen. Click the chat caption of your choice to submit the text to the chat.

 If someone is bothering or annoying you, you can ignore that person by selecting his or her name from the list of chat users at the right and then clicking the Ignore toolbar button.

7 To chat privately with a member of the chat group, select the person from the list of chat users, click Member, and then click Whisper Box to open a private chat box, as shown in Figure 8-10.

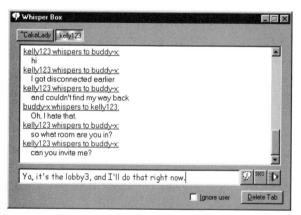

FIGURE 8-10

Use the Whisper Box to conduct a private conversation with someone.

8 To exit the chat room, choose the Room menu's Leave command.

9 To continue chatting, choose the Room menu's Room List command to display the list of chat rooms and then select another room.

 To send a file to someone, select the person's name from the list of chat users, choose the Member menu's Send File command, select the file, and then click Open.

Using mIRC for IRC

A popular **shareware** IRC client that you can use to chat on IRC servers on the Internet is known as mIRC. (The "m" stands for the name of the author who wrote the program.) You can download the program from *http://www.mirc.com* or from *http://www.download.com*, where you can also download other IRC clients to try out if you like. You don't need to use mIRC to benefit from reading this section—most IRC clients work similarly.

Starting mIRC and Joining a Chat Room

After you download and install mIRC, start mIRC and join a chat room by following these steps:

1 Click the Start button, choose Programs, choose mIRC, and then click mIRC32. The first time you start mIRC, you select a chat server and enter your user information in the mIRC Options dialog box that displays (see Figure 8-11).

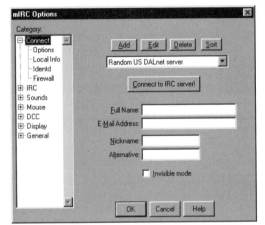

FIGURE 8-11

Use the mIRC Options dialog box to connect to a chat server.

2 Select a chat server from the drop-down list box.

3 Enter a name and the **e-mail** information about yourself that you want other chat users to see.

4 When you're finished, click Connect To IRC Server! to display a list of channels (rooms) that you can join, as shown in Figure 8-12.

FIGURE 8-12

Use the mIRC Channels Folder dialog box to select the chat channel you want to join.

5 Select a channel from the list, and then click Join to enter the chat channel, as shown in Figure 8-13.

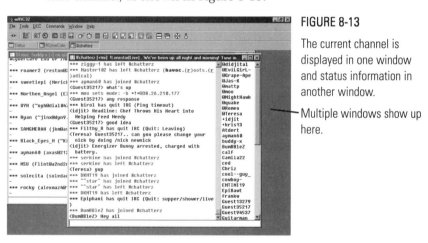

FIGURE 8-13

The current channel is displayed in one window and status information in another window.

Multiple windows show up here.

6 If you want to open another channel, click the Channels Folder toolbar button to display the mIRC Channels Folder dialog box.

Chatting with mIRC

To chat on an IRC channel that you've joined, follow these steps:

1   Enter a chat channel.

2   Type your text in the text box at the bottom of the channel window, and press Enter.

3   To chat privately with someone, double-click the person's name in the list of chat users to open a private chat window (see Figure 8-14). Enter text in the private chat window just as you would in a channel.

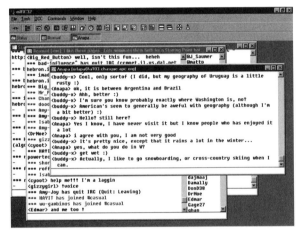

FIGURE 8-14

Double-click a person's name in the list of chat users to chat privately with that person.

 If someone is bothering or annoying you, you can ignore the person by right-clicking his or her name in the list of chat users, choosing Control, and then clicking Ignore. If someone is behaving inappropriately for the channel, you can also use the Control submenu to Kick the person (kick the person out of the channel) or Ban and Kick the person (kick the person out of the channel and prevent him or her from returning).

4   If you want to send a file to someone, choose the DCC menu's Send command, enter the person's nickname in the Nick box, select the file, and click Send.

5   To disconnect from the chat server when you're finished chatting, click the Disconnect From IRC Server toolbar button.

Using ICQ

ICQ is an extremely popular, free program that you can use to send messages to people you know without your having to join a chat room or channel. If you have ICQ running while you're connected to the Internet, your friends and associates can look in their Contact Lists, see that you're online, and send you an instant message or open up a chat window with you.

To use ICQ, download it from *http://www.icq.com* and install it on your computer by running the setup file and then following the directions provided. If you don't have an ICQ account, you are prompted to enter your e-mail address and any information you would like to be made publicly available, such as your name, e-mail address, personal interests, and so on.

Starting ICQ and Viewing Your Contacts

After you install ICQ, the program starts automatically and a small flower icon appears in the lower right corner of your desktop, as shown in Figure 8-15. If it doesn't appear, click the Start button, choose Programs, choose ICQ, and then click ICQ.

FIGURE 8-15

Double-click the flower icon to open ICQ.

To use ICQ, follow these steps:

1   Double-click the flower icon found near the right end of the Windows taskbar to display the ICQ program window that shows your ICQ Contact List (see Figure 8-16).

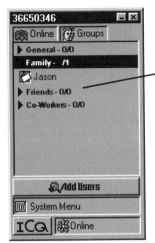

FIGURE 8-16

The ICQ program window lets you view your Contact List and see who's currently online.

This is a list of ICQ contacts.

2 Click Groups. This shifts your view back and forth between groups and a list of your **contacts.**

3 Click Online. This shifts your view back and forth between all of your contacts and only those currently online.

4 For information about a contact, click the contact and then choose Info from the pop-up menu to display the user information for the contact, as shown in Figure 8-17.

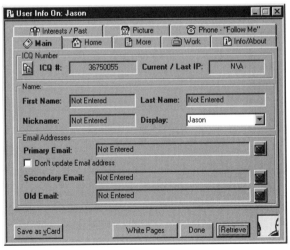

FIGURE 8-17

An ICQ contact.

5 Optionally, click Save As **vCard,** and use the Save As dialog box to export the contact information to an e-mail program such as **Microsoft Outlook Express** or **Netscape Messenger.**

6 Click Done when you're finished viewing the contact.

Adding Contacts

Before you begin using ICQ, you need to add names to your Contact List so that you have some people with whom you can chat. To find names and add them to your ICQ Contact List, follow these steps:

1 Double-click the flower icon found near the right end of the Windows taskbar to open ICQ.

2 Click Add Users to display the dialog box shown in Figure 8-18.

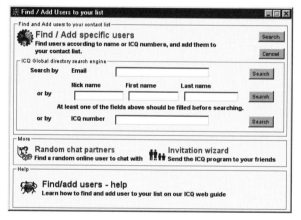

FIGURE 8-18

Use the Find/Add Users To Your List dialog box to search for people to add to your Contact List.

3 To search for someone you know who uses ICQ, enter the person's e-mail address, nickname, name, or ICQ number in the appropriate box and click Search.

4 ICQ lists the names of people who match your search criteria. Double-click a name to add the person to your Contact List.

5 If the person you found requires authorization to be added to your Contact List, type a short message asking for permission to add his or her name to your list and then click Request.

6 If the person doesn't require authorization, choose a group for the contact when prompted and click OK.

7 Close any open dialog boxes when you're finished searching for people.

Sending a Message

Once you've established a list of contacts, you can send an instant message (a simplified, speedy e-mail) to anyone currently online who's listed in your Contact List. To do so, follow these steps:

1   Double-click the flower icon found near the right end of the Windows taskbar to open ICQ.

2   Click Online to display all your contacts who are currently online. Double-click the name of the contact with whom you want to talk. ICQ opens the Send Online Message window (see Figure 8-19).

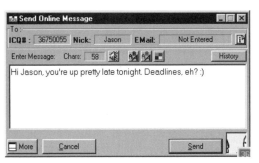

FIGURE 8-19

Type a short message in the Send Online Message window, and then click Send.

3   Type a short message in the box, and click Send to deliver the message.

 Messages are great for quick comments that don't require much or any feedback. If you want to carry on a conversation, however, use ICQ Chat instead.

Receiving a Message

When someone sends you a message with ICQ, the flower icon changes to a note icon and flashes. Double-click the note icon to display the message. To reply to the message or forward it to another user, click Reply or Forward, type your message, and then click Send. If you want to chat with the person, click Request A Chat, enter a chat subject, and then click Chat.

Using ICQ Chat

If someone comes online with whom you want to have a conversation, use ICQ's Chat. This chat option allows you to have a real-time conversation. To set up a chat session with a contact who is currently online, follow these steps:

1   Double-click the flower icon found near the right end of the Windows taskbar to open ICQ.

2   Click Online to display all your contacts who are currently online. Click the name of the contact with whom you want to talk, and then choose ICQ Chat from the pop-up menu.

3   Enter a chat subject in the Send Online Chat Request dialog box, and then click Chat. When the recipient accepts the chat request, ICQ opens a Chat window (see Figure 8-20).

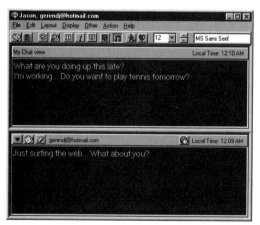

FIGURE 8-20

Use the ICQ Chat window like a normal chat program to converse with someone.

Notes   *ICQ might ask whether you want to use a Split Mode or an IRC Mode window for your chat. Choose Split Mode if you're carrying on a real-time conversation with someone so that you can see what he or she is typing as it's being typed. Otherwise, use the IRC Mode to leave a window open for occasional messages to and from the person with whom you're chatting.*

4   Close the window when you're finished chatting.

When someone sends you a Chat Request, the flower icon turns into a flashing quote balloon. Double-click the balloon icon to display the Chat Request box. Click Accept to begin chatting.

Changing Your Online Status and Profile

ICQ lets you change your online status as well as your contact information, known as a personal profile. This privacy feature lets you decide when you're available and what kind of information about yourself that others can view.

To change your online status, right-click the flower icon, choose Online Status from the shortcut menu, and then click either Available/Connect or Offline/Disconnect.

To modify your personal profile, follow these steps:

1 Double-click the flower icon found near the right end of the Windows taskbar to open ICQ.

2 Click ICQ, choose Add/Change Current User from the pop-up menu, and then click View/Change My Details, as shown in Figure 8-21.

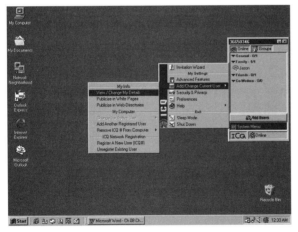

FIGURE 8-21

Modify your personal profile.

3 Use the various tabs to enter information about yourself, and click Save when you're finished.

 Entering more information helps your friends find you in the ICQ database. However, all the information you enter is visible to anyone on the Internet, so don't add information that you don't want people to see.

Using Yahoo! Chat

Yahoo! Chat is a free Web-based chat service that's very much like IRC on the Web. Most web-based chat services work in a similar fashion, so even if you use another chat service, this section will still help you with the basics.

Joining a Chat Room

To join a Yahoo! Chat room, follow these steps:

1 Start your web browser, and then go to *http://www.yahoo.com.*

2 Click the Chat **hyperlink.** Unless you have saved your settings with Yahoo! Chat, you're asked to either log in or sign up for a new account.

3 If you don't have a Yahoo! Chat account, click the Sign Me Up hyperlink. Otherwise, enter your user name and password, and click Sign In.

4 If you chose to sign up for a new account, first read and accept Yahoo! Chat's Terms Of Service agreement.

5 On the next web page, choose a Yahoo! ID that you want to use while online, enter a password, and fill in any personal information you want to make available on the Internet. Click Submit This Form when you're finished.

6 After you sign up or sign in, Yahoo! Chat displays the Welcome To Yahoo! Chat page, which looks similar to the page shown in Figure 8-22.

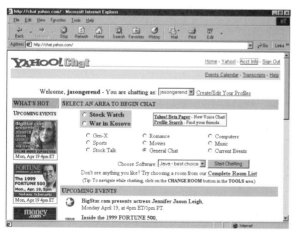

FIGURE 8-22

The Welcome page you see when you start Yahoo! Chat looks similar to this page.

7 Select a category by clicking the option button in front of the category, and then click Start Chatting. Yahoo! Chat loads and displays the chat room you selected (see Figure 8-23).

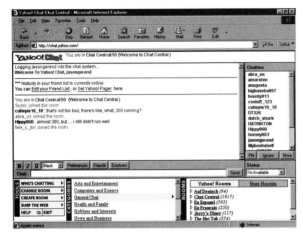

FIGURE 8-23

A chat room in Yahoo! Chat.

8 To change rooms, click the Change Room link in the Tools section of the window and then click a category link in the Categories section to display the rooms in that category. Click a room's name in the Rooms section to join the chat room.

 Click the User Rooms link to display the chat rooms created by users.

9 To exit the chat room, click Exit in the Tools section.

 To create your own chat room, click the Create Room link in the Tools section, enter a name and welcome message, and then click Create My Room.

Chatting with Yahoo! Chat

After you join a chat room, it's time to do some chatting. You can use Yahoo! Chat to talk to all of the people in the room, or you can send private messages to individuals.

To use Yahoo! Chat to converse in a chat room, follow these steps:

1 Enter a chat room.

2 To say something in the room, enter text in the Chat box found near the bottom of the window.

 To ignore someone, select the person's name in the Chatters list and then click Ignore.

3 To send an emotion icon with your text, click Emotions, select an emotion or action from the list, and click Emote User.

 If you want to change your status in the chat room—for example, to let users know that you're dashing out for a quick cup of coffee—select a status from the Status drop-down list box located under the Chatters list.

4 To chat privately with someone, double-click a name in the Chatters list to open a PM (Personal Message) dialog box, as shown in Figure 8-24.

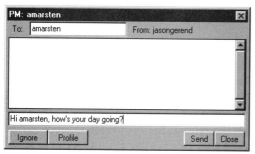

FIGURE 8-24

Use the PM dialog box to carry on a private conversation with someone.

Using AOL Instant Messenger

Netscape Navigator now comes with a popular chat client used by America Online members called AOL Instant Messenger. AOL Instant Messenger works much like ICQ, described earlier in the chapter.

Setting Up AOL Instant Messenger

To set up AOL Instant Messenger, follow these steps:

1 Click the Start button, choose Programs, choose Netscape Communicator, and click AOL Instant Messenger.

2 In the dialog box shown in Figure 8-25, click Sign On.

FIGURE 8-25

The Sign On dialog box.

3 Click Register New Screen Name to open Netscape Navigator and display the web page shown in Figure 8-26.

 If you're an AOL member, you can click Use AOL Screen Name to use your existing AOL screen name.

FIGURE 8-26

Registering a new screen name.

If you know other people who use AOL Instant Messenger, you can add them to your Buddies, Family, or Co-Workers list so that you can easily send these contacts messages without needing to enter their screen names. To add a person to a list, follow these steps:

1   Click the Start button, choose Programs, choose Netscape Communicator, and click AOL Instant Messenger to start AOL Instant Messenger.

2   In your Buddies List window, click the List Setup tab, as shown in Figure 8-27.

FIGURE 8-27

The List Setup tab of the Buddies List window.

3   If you know a person's AOL Instant Messenger screen name, you can add the person to a list by selecting a folder (Buddies, Family, or Co-Workers), clicking Add A Buddy, and typing the screen name in the box provided.

If you don't know a person's AOL Instant Messenger screen name, you can search for the person by choosing the People menu's Find A Buddy command and then choosing one of the submenu's commands. Use the boxes provided to enter the information you know about the person.

By default, if people know your e-mail address, they can find your screen name. If you want people to be able to search for you by your real name or address, choose the File menu's My Profile command. Then select the Allow People To Search For Me check box, and enter information about yourself in the boxes. Click Next to describe your interest areas, and click Next again to enter more information about yourself. Note that this information becomes public to AOL Instant Messenger users, so you might not want to enter your complete address. Also, be aware that if you allow people to search for you, you will probably receive more chat requests.

Chatting

When you start AOL Instant Messenger and display the Online tab of your Buddies List window, as shown in Figure 8-28, you can see whether any of the people you've added to your lists are currently online. If someone is, you can select that person and click Send Instant Message. When you do, AOL Instant Messenger opens the window shown in Figure 8-29, which you use to correspond with the other person.

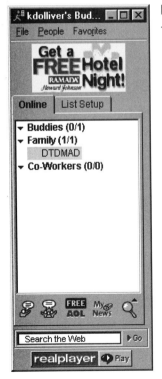

FIGURE 8-28

The Online tab of the Buddies List window.

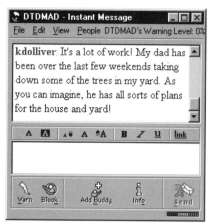

FIGURE 8-29

The Instant Message window.

 To send a message to someone not on one of your lists, just click Send Instant Message and enter the person's screen name in the To box.

Use the list box at the bottom of the window to type your messages, and click Send. The messages you send, along with the messages you receive, are displayed in the box at the top.

If you receive a message that offends or annoys you, click Warn. If you want to block all correspondence from the person, click Block.

 To format the text you send, use the Formatting toolbar buttons.

To change your Instant Messenger settings, choose the File menu's My Options command and then choose Preferences from the submenu. For example, click the Controls tab to specify who can contact you, whether or not they can see how long you've been idle, and what information people can access about you if they know your e-mail address.

CHAPTER 9

The Rest of the Net

The other chapters in this book focus on a handful of the most popular **Internet** activities. You should know, however, that because the Internet is constantly growing and evolving, people are doing a wide variety of new things with it all the time. This chapter introduces three other activities you can do on the Internet:

- Playing games online
- Using **Telnet**
- Browsing **FTP** sites

Playing Games Online

From the advent of Pong back in the mid-1970s, software developers have been dreaming of a world of virtual reality, a world in which computer users could test skills and ideas through interactivity. With every passing day, developers of online games are getting closer to making this dream a reality. Just about every type of game you can imagine now has multiplayer capabilities over the Internet, and a multitude of Internet game services have sprung up to provide opportunities for people to play games with one another. There are now hundreds of different online and retail games. This section briefly describes the different types of games and game services available and then demonstrates how to start a couple of games using game services.

Understanding the Types of Internet Games

Games can interface with the Internet in a number of different ways: through game services, as online games (either as a part of a game service or by itself), by retail games that directly interface with a game service without using a **web browser**, and by retail games with subscription services to their associated online communities. The most popular method of finding players on the Internet and joining games is by using

9

a game service such as Mplayer.com or MSN Gaming Zone. To use a game service, go to its **web site,** sign up to become a member (often for free), and then go to the game room that has the game you want to play. Figure 9-1 shows the lobby of a game room at Mplayer.com.

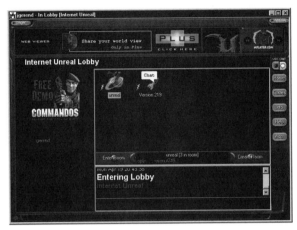

FIGURE 9-1

The lobby of a game room at Mplayer.com.

Inside the game room, people are playing the game or waiting to start a new game. You can either join an existing game or start a new game and invite people to join you. The types of games offered vary with the game service, but they generally include a number of popular retail games from each genre, free Web-based games such as Blackjack and Chess, and sometimes a few premium games that you need to pay extra to play.

Online games are small games that are part of a **web page,** usually in the form of a **Java** applet or a Shockwave control. Both of these options are generally part of your web browser. These simple arcade or card games are usually part of game services, but you can also find many games scattered on various sites throughout the Internet.

Some newer retail games, such as Half Life (shown in Figure 9-2), UnReal Tournament, and others, include a built-in **server** browser to allow you to find a game server and join another game without leaving your current game. These games generally use a game service to maintain a directory of game servers and thus can be used either from within a game or externally by using a game service's web site or a program such as GameSpy.

FIGURE 9-2

An in-game server browser lets you find another game and start playing without leaving your current game.

Retail games with online communities in which you interact are another type of Internet game that has grown in popularity. In these games, usually of the role-playing genre, thousands of people interact in an online world. You generally need to purchase this type of game and then pay monthly dues to access the online community. Examples of this type of game are Everquest and Ultima Online.

Using an Online Game Service

To demonstrate how to use an online game service, the following section uses Mplayer.com as an example. Many other game services are available, and you might want to use a different one, but they all work in a similar fashion.

To start using Mplayer.com, follow these steps:

1 Open your web browser, and enter the **URL** *http://www.mplayer.com.*

2 Click the Free Signup **hyperlink** if you don't already have an account.

3 Enter your user name in the Choose A Member Name box.

4 Fill out the rest of the signup **form**, and then click Accept And Install to **download** the program to your hard drive and install it.

5 To start Mplayer.com after you finish installing, click the Start button, choose Programs, choose Mplayer.com, and then click Connect To Mplayer.com.

6 In the Mplayer.com window, shown in Figure 9-3, click Play Now or Login Here.

FIGURE 9-3

The Mplayer.com web site.

7 On the right side of the window, click Games to display a list of game categories.

8 Scroll down until you find the category or game you want to play, and then click its hyperlink to enter the lobby for the game. (You might have to go through several pages before you get there.)

A lobby is where players gather to join up in a game or browse a list of currently active games.

9 Once you're in the lobby for the game you want to play, select a room and then click Enter Room. This takes you into a game room, as shown in Figure 9-4.

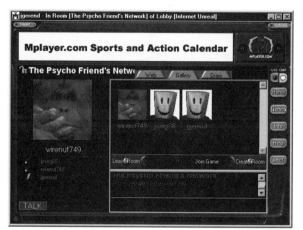

FIGURE 9-4

A game room at Mplayer.com.

10 Click Talk to talk with the other members of the room, or click Join Game to start playing.

 To shift the Mplayer software between web-surfing mode, in which you can view web pages, and chat mode, in which you can view game rooms, click Web or Chat on the right side of the window.

Playing an Online Game at Yahoo! Games

Online games are played vastly differently, depending on what the game is and who created it. However, the process of finding and starting a game is similar whether it's Backgammon on Yahoo! Games or Chess on the MSN Gaming Zone. This section demonstrates how to find and play a simple online game using Yahoo! Games as an example.

To find a game and start playing it on Yahoo! Games, follow these steps:

1 Open your web browser, and enter the URL *http://www.yahoo.com*.

2 Click the Games hyperlink to display a listing of games available, as shown in Figure 9-5.

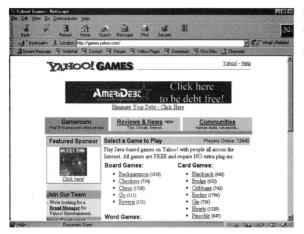

FIGURE 9-5

The list of games at Yahoo! Games.

3 Click a game's name. If you aren't a member of Yahoo!, click the Sign Me Up link to get a free membership to Yahoo! before continuing. (You need to be a member to play the games. If you have already signed up for another Yahoo! Service such as Mail or Auctions, you can use that membership user ID and password.)

4 Depending on the game, click a category to select a level of difficulty.

5 Click a room's name to enter the game room. Yahoo! Games then loads the game program that you use to join a game and chat with other users, as shown in Figure 9-6.

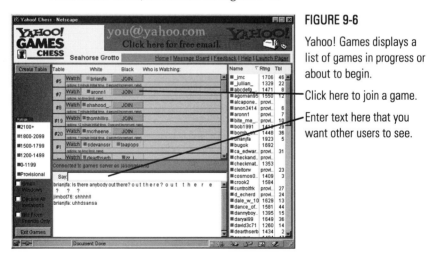

FIGURE 9-6

Yahoo! Games displays a list of games in progress or about to begin.

Click here to join a game.

Enter text here that you want other users to see.

6 Enter text in the Say box to send a message to other users in the room.

7 Click Join at the table at which you want to begin playing.

8 Click Start to begin playing your game, as shown in Figure 9-7.

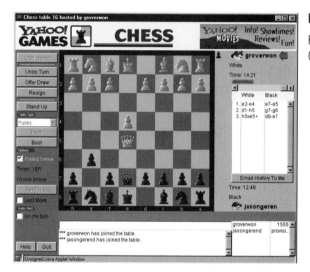

FIGURE 9-7

Playing chess at Yahoo! Games.

9 Click Quit when you're finished.

Using Telnet

If online games give you a feel for the future of the Internet, Telnet gives you a feel for its past. Telnet allows you to turn your computer into a terminal, which is hardly more than a monitor and a keyboard. Once your terminal is set up, you can log on to a remote computer to browse text-based information. Telnet started as a way for users, especially at universities, to log onto older, expensive mainframe computers. As time goes on, the number of uses for the Telnet protocol will decrease. But because many library catalogs are not yet available for browsing on the World Wide Web, they can still be browsed using a terminal set up to Telnet standards. To start a Telnet session, you can either download a Telnet utility or use the Telnet accessory that comes with Microsoft Windows. This section describes how to access Telnet sites and how to work with the Windows Telnet accessory.

Starting a Telnet Session

Telnet is designed to allow access to mainframe computers in remote locations. It is still in common use for archives such as public libraries. Before you can begin Telnetting, you need to find out the following information about the remote computer:

- A user account to access the remote computer. If you need an account, you need to contact the **network** administrator for the computer.

- The dial-up number to connect to the mainframe computer. This is generally available only from the network administrator for the computer. Alternatively, you need access to a web page with a Telnet access point. See the tip on page 179 for more information.

- Details on the protocol that's used. If the mainframe computer does *not* use a protocol called TCP/IP, which is the normal Internet communications protocol on the Telnet connection, you need to consult the network administrator for the remote computer for help.

- The host name of the Telnet access point.

You can access a Telnet site in one of two ways: by starting the Telnet accessory and connecting to the resource directly or by using your web browser and clicking a Telnet hyperlink on a web page to start the Telnet accessory and make the connection. Normally you see "**http://**" in the Address or Location box of your web browser. After you successfully hook up to a Telnet mainframe, you'll see "telnet://<hostname>" in the Address or Location box of your web browser. If you know the host name of the Telnet site, you can make a direct connection by following these steps:

1 Connect to the Internet or the dial-up number for the mainframe.

2 Start the Telnet accessory by double-clicking the telnet application file in Windows Explorer or My Computer. (This file is usually located in the Windows folder.) Alternatively, click the Start button and choose Run. Then type *telnet* in the Open box, and press Enter.

3 Choose the Connect menu's Remote System command to display the dialog box shown in Figure 9-8.

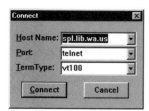

FIGURE 9-8

The Connect dialog box.

4   Enter the host name in the Host Name box. If you've visited the site before, you can select it from the drop-down list box.

5   Verify that the port is set to Telnet and that the term type is set to vt100.

6   Click Connect. The Telnet window displays the opening screen of information, which often includes a login prompt, as shown in Figure 9-9. If you don't have a user name or password, see whether the site offers a way for you to log on as a guest.

FIGURE 9-9

Beginning a Telnet session.

If you don't know the host name of the resource to which you want to connect, you can use your web browser to start Telnet and connect to the resource. To do so, follow these steps:

1   Start your web browser, and display the web page with the link to the Telnet resource.

2   Click the hyperlink to the resource to open the Telnet accessory and connect to the resource.

 To search or browse lists of various Telnet sites, you can go to the web page at http://www.lights.com/hytelnet/. *This site also includes basic directions for working with the Telnet sites it lists.*

Working with Telnet

Every Telnet site works a little differently, so any general instructions would never apply to all sites. However, the following tips might help you navigate Telnet sites:

- If the screen looks funny and is difficult to read, your terminal emulation might be incorrect. Terminal emulation refers to the type of terminal your computer imitates when it connects to the Telnet site. To change your terminal emulation, choose the Terminal menu's Preferences command and click one of the Emulation option buttons (see Figure 9-10). VT-100/ANSI is the most common, so choose this emulation unless you are told otherwise or if you just can't get the connection to work.

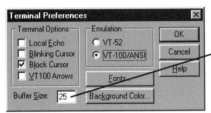

FIGURE 9-10

Setting preferences in Telnet.

Enter a value here to describe how many lines you want to display in the Telnet window.

- If every letter you type is repeated, turn off the local echo by choosing the Terminal menu's Preferences command and clearing the Local Echo check box.

- You move through information using the Telnet accessory by pressing keys on the keyboard instead of by using the mouse. When you enter a command, this command is executed on the remote computer (the Telnet site to which you're connected). For instance, you might press the Spacebar to tell the Telnet site to display the next page of information. Often, you use the arrow keys to move through pages of information. If you have a question, see whether the site provides a command you can type to access help; for example, you might need to type a question mark and then press Enter, as shown in Figure 9-11. On many systems, prompts are available in the middle or at the bottom of the screen to explain the command options you can use.

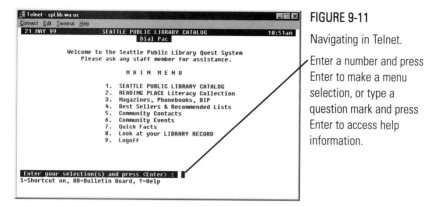

FIGURE 9-11

Navigating in Telnet.

Enter a number and press Enter to make a menu selection, or type a question mark and press Enter to access help information.

- To end a Telnet session, choose the Connect menu's Disconnect command.

Browsing FTP Sites

FTP stands for File Transfer Protocol, and the name of this protocol describes what it's used for—transferring files. You use FTP sites to download files or to upload files for others to download. FTP sites aren't as much fun to browse as web sites, but they do contain a great amount of information you might want to access. Unfortunately, finding the site you're looking for and the file you want can be a challenge. This section describes how to search FTP sites for files and how to navigate the FTP site structure.

Finding FTP Files

If you're looking for a file that you suspect is on an FTP site, often the easiest way to get to the file is by performing a web search as described in Chapter 4. Web pages often have hyperlinks to FTP sites for downloading files. However, you can also search FTP sites directly if you know the name of the particular file you want.

 For a list of anonymous FTP sites, visit ftp://rtfm.mit.edu:/pub/usenet-by-group/news.answers/ftp-list/sitelist/.

9

If you know the name of the file you want to download, you can use a **search engine** such as Lycos to search FTP sites. To do so, follow these steps:

1 Enter *http://ftpsearch.lycos.com/* in the Address or Location box of your web browser to display a web page such as the one shown in Figure 9-12.

FIGURE 9-12

Performing an FTP search using Lycos.

  *Click the Advanced hyperlink to perform an advanced search, which allows you to limit variables such as the file size, the **domain name** of the source, or the category of file (such as the **operating system**).*

2 In the File Name Or Keyword box, enter the name of the file of which you want a copy.

3 If you know the file type, select it from the drop-down list box.

4 Click Go Get It. Lycos returns a list of files that match your criteria (see Figure 9-13).

FIGURE 9-13

A list of files found on public FTP sites.

5 If you see the file you want on several sites, look for the site that is physically closest to you. (Many lists of FTP sites include their physical location. Where possible, check the country's domain to pick a site in your own country.) Click the filename at the far end of the FTP path hyperlink (in the example shown, family.exe) to display your web browser's download dialog box, as shown in Figure 9-14.

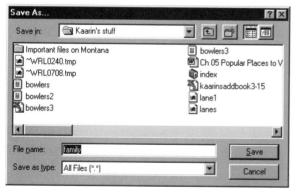

FIGURE 9-14

Netscape Navigator's Save As dialog box.

Despite what you might have heard, physical distance still makes a difference when you are navigating through http:// or ftp:// sites on the Internet. When you travel on the Information Superhighway, there are still a number of relatively narrow roads. The farther that your information has to travel, the more likely that it will have to travel on a narrow road and run into a traffic jam.

Navigating FTP Sites

If you know the URL of an FTP site, you can browse the site using your web browser much the way you browse folders on your computer using Windows Explorer or My Computer. To browse an FTP site using Internet Explorer, follow these steps:

1   Enter the FTP site's URL in the Address box, as shown in Figure 9-15.

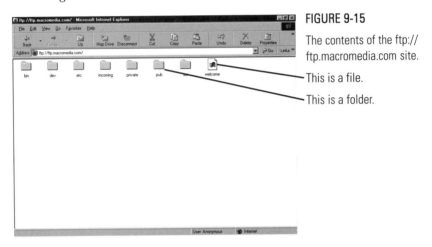

FIGURE 9-15

The contents of the ftp:// ftp.macromedia.com site.

This is a file.

This is a folder.

2   To display the contents of a folder in a new window, double-click that folder. To move back to a folder's parent folder, look for a hyperlink that reads something like Up To Higher-Level Directory. On some sites, the hyperlink to get to a higher-level directory is just a double period (..). The actual words in the hyperlink will vary by FTP site.

3   To open a text file in a new window, double-click the text file. To open or download other types of files, double-click them. When Internet Explorer displays the File Download dialog box (see Figure 9-16), click the Save This File To Disk option button to download the file and then click OK.

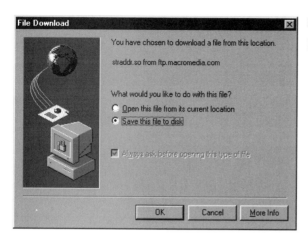

FIGURE 9-16

Downloading a file.

 Use the View menu's Large Icons, Small Icons, List, and Details commands to change the way Internet Explorer displays folders and files. Use the View menu's Arrange Icons commands to sort folders and files by name, type, size, or date.

To browse an FTP site using **Netscape Navigator**, follow these steps:

1 Enter the FTP site's URL in the Location box, as shown in Figure 9-17.

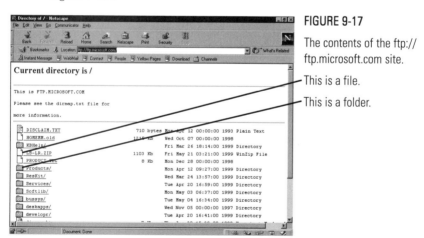

FIGURE 9-17

The contents of the ftp:// ftp.microsoft.com site.

This is a file.

This is a folder.

2 To display the contents of a folder, click the folder's hyperlink. To read a text file, click the file's hyperlink. Netscape Navigator displays the text of the file, as shown in Figure 9-18.

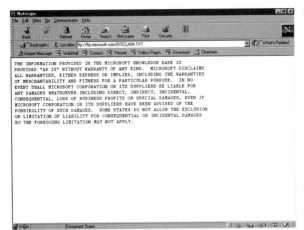

FIGURE 9-18

A text file on an FTP site.

3 To download other types of files, click the file's hyperlink. Netscape Navigator displays the Save As dialog box so that you can specify a storage location for the file.

CHAPTER 10

A Web-Publishing Primer

Web publishing isn't the way it used to be. In the beginning, creating a **web page** was tedious and time-consuming. Web designers had to make web pages by hand, typing lines of code in front of everything they created—text, **hyperlinks**, images—you get the idea.

Times have changed. Now anyone can create web pages that put to shame the pages that were labored over in the old days. And the process is easy, too. This chapter explains how to get started in web publishing by covering the following topics:

- Obtaining a **web site**
- Selecting a web-publishing program
- Using FrontPage Express
- Using **Netscape Composer**

Obtaining a Web Site

Finding a web site to call your own might seem tough at first. If your **ISP** gives you free space for a web site (usually between 2 MB and 10 MB), the solution is simple: use the site you already have available to you. If your ISP doesn't provide you with a free web site, you need to either pay for a site or obtain a free site from one of the companies that offer web sites at no charge.

Using a Web Site from Your ISP

Many ISPs give you free space on their **servers** to store your web site. If you have an ISP that gives you a free web site, take it. While it's likely that the amount of server space provided is fairly small (perhaps only 2 MB), it's an excellent place to start, and most ISPs will increase your server space for a fee if you outgrow your initial allotment. The benefits of using your ISP to host (or store) your web site include cost (assuming you don't pay extra for the service), customer service (some, but not all,

ISPs will help you with any problems you have configuring your web site), and perhaps extra features, such as support for Microsoft FrontPage Server Extensions. Your ISP may also support virtual domain hosting for an additional fee; you can then choose your own web site name, for example, www.yourname.com.

Using a Free Web Site

If a free web site from your ISP is not an option for you, the next best way to get started making web pages is to create your web site with a company that provides free web sites. Free web sites benefit from being included in a company's member directory. With some free web site companies placing in the top 10 of the most accessed web sites on the **Internet**, the potentially high number of visitors to your site can be a compelling feature. Most free web site providers also provide easy-to-use tools or templates to help you create basic to moderately complex web pages, as well as lots of free graphics. However, it's often difficult to create more advanced web pages using the tools they provide. It can also be difficult to publish on your web site pages that you created with tools different from the **online** tools the company uses.

How do companies make money giving away free web sites? By advertising on each and every web site they give away (see Figure 10-1).

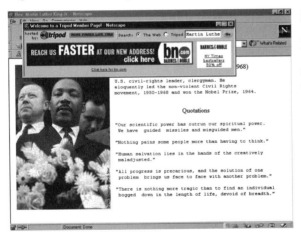

FIGURE 10-1

A free home page on Tripod, with the Tripod advertising banner displayed over the page.

Companies advertise on web pages in slightly different ways. Some create small browser windows that automatically open with an advertisement, some place an ad across the top or bottom of your pages, and some supplement one of these approaches by placing their company logo in one corner of your page—always visible onscreen. In any case, the advertisers who use some of your space are paying for your free web site. Oftentimes, you can purchase more disk space and even remove the ads from your site for a fee.

If you have existing web pages, or you want to use more powerful tools than those provided by the company, make sure the company you sign up with supports using File Transfer Protocol (**FTP**), Hypertext Transfer Protocol (**HTTP**) upload, and CGI Scripts or FrontPage Server Extensions to publish your pages. The following companies offer free web sites:

- AngelFire
- GeoCities
- Homestead
- Hometown AOL
- theglobe.com
- Tripod
- Xoom.com

Paying for a Web Site

If your ISP can't meet your web site needs and a free web site doesn't offer what you want, you can pay a company to host your web site. Paying for your web site provides a fair number of advantages. You usually get a larger disk-space allotment than you would from your ISP or a free web site provider. You also get a variety of features you may or may not need, such as FrontPage Server Extensions (useful only if you have Microsoft FrontPage or Microsoft Office 2000), multiple **e-mail** addresses, your own **domain name** (for example, *www.stephenlnelson.com*), and various business-oriented features. You'll still need an ISP to provide you with Internet access in most cases.

 Notes To register a domain name, go to the Network Solutions web site at http://www.networksolutions.com. *Enter the domain name you'd like, select the domain name type (.com, .net, or .org), and click Go to see whether that name is available. Registering a domain name currently costs $70 and the registration is valid for two years.*

10

Selecting a Web-Publishing Program

It's hard to go wrong in selecting a program to use for your first forays into web publishing. However, quite a few programs are available, and not all of them will appeal to you. This section explains how these programs work and describes the general categories of web-authoring programs.

 Notes *The remainder of this chapter focuses on using **Microsoft FrontPage Express** and Netscape Composer. If you want to use a different program, don't worry. Most of the techniques covered here work similarly for other programs of this type.*

At the heart of any web-authoring program is a text editor. Web pages are really nothing but text documents with some special codes (called **HTML** markup) to tell the **web browser** how to display the text, so it makes sense that these programs are based on text editors. You could even use the simple Notepad program that comes with **Microsoft Windows** to create your web pages. However, if you did use a text editor such as Notepad, you would have to manually type in the entire HTML markup yourself—a time-consuming task that requires patience and a good book on HTML.

Some web-authoring programs go a step further by letting you choose the codes you want to include instead of making you type them yourself. This both speeds the process of creating pages and makes it easier if you're unfamiliar with codes. These powerful programs allow you to create pages exactly the way you want them, and they feature all the latest bells and whistles; however, they're usually more difficult to use if you're a beginner. Examples of this type of program are HotDog Pro and HomeSite.

What You See Is What You Get (WYSIWYG) editors let you create web pages just as you would a word-processor document or a desktop-publishing file. The program creates all the code for you. (Many programs permit HTML markup and even help you modify it.) FrontPage Express (included with Microsoft Internet Explorer) and Netscape Composer (included with **Netscape Communicator**) are two examples of WYSIWYG editors.

If you have a free web site, the company hosting your web site will probably provide you with a web-based web page editor. These editors typically consist of either sample web pages that you can modify with your own text and graphics or form-based editors that ask you a series of questions and then create a page based on your answers (see Figure 10-2).

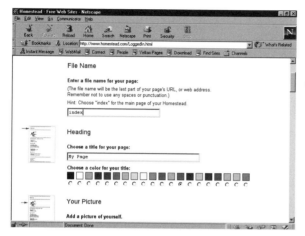

FIGURE 10-2

Form-based web-authoring programs ask you a series of questions and then build your page for you.

Some companies are now creating actual online WYSIWYG programs that you can use in almost the same way as stand-alone editors, such as FrontPage Express or Netscape Composer. These editors are almost always limited in their ability to create complex pages, but they usually do a good job of walking you through the process of creating your first web pages (see Figure 10-3).

FIGURE 10-3

Some companies now offer their own basic web-authoring programs, such as this one from Homestead.

If your web site doesn't support publishing your web pages using FTP, HTTP upload, CGI Scripts, or FrontPage Server Extensions, you'll need to use the tools provided for you to create at least some of your web pages.

Even if you have a free web site that doesn't support publishing files from a web-authoring program, you can usually still use pages you create in one of the less fully featured stand-alone web-authoring programs.

Using FrontPage Express

FrontPage Express is a free version of Microsoft's professional web-authoring and web site management program, FrontPage. Although it lacks many of the advanced features of FrontPage and a couple of the not-so-advanced features—such as a spelling checker and sample web pages—it's a very powerful program that is every bit as useful for beginners as it is for advanced web authors. In fact, it's really much too powerful to cover completely in this overview of web publishing, so if you don't see the feature you need covered in this chapter, play around a little with the program—you'll be surprised at how much you can accomplish by experimenting.

 One bonus of using FrontPage Express is that the process of creating pages in the full version of FrontPage is almost identical, making it easy to move up to a more powerful program as your needs become more sophisticated.

Installing and Opening FrontPage Express

FrontPage Express is included with Windows 98 or newer, as well as with Internet Explorer 4.0 or newer. To start the program, click the Start button, choose Programs, choose Accessories, choose Internet Tools, and then click FrontPage Express. The program is not always installed by default, however. If you find that FrontPage Express isn't installed on your system, install it by following these steps:

1 Click the Start button, choose Settings, and then click Control Panel.

2 Double-click the Add/Remove Programs icon to display the dialog box shown in Figure 10-4.

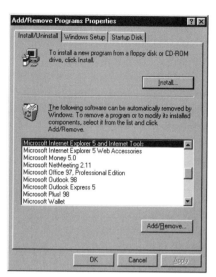

FIGURE 10-4

The Add/Remove Programs Properties dialog box.

3   Click the Windows Setup tab.

4   In the Components box, double-click Internet Tools to open the Internet Tools dialog box.

5   Select the check box next to FrontPage Express, and click OK.

6   Click OK again to close the Add/Remove Programs Properties dialog box. If necessary, you will be prompted to insert your Windows Installation CD-ROM.

7   To start FrontPage Express after installing, click the Start button, choose Programs, choose Accessories, choose Internet Tools, and then click FrontPage Express.

 Notes   *The installation process might be slightly different, depending on which version of Internet Explorer you have.*

Opening Pages

To open a web page, click the Open File toolbar button, and then click Browse to locate the page on your computer (see Figure 10-5). If the page is on the Internet, click the From Location option button in the Open File dialog box and enter the **URL** for the page in the text box.

FIGURE 10-5

In the Open File dialog box, tell FrontPage Express where the page you want to edit is located.

Creating a Page from a Template or Wizard

FrontPage Express comes with several templates and **wizards** that are extremely useful for quickly and easily creating your first pages. To create a page from a template or wizard, choose the File menu's New command, select the form or wizard you want to use from the New Page dialog box, and click OK (see Figure 10-6).

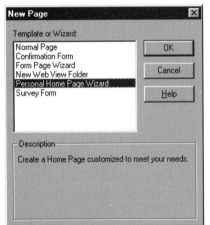

FIGURE 10-6

Use the New Page dialog box to choose a template or wizard to help you get started creating your web page.

If you choose a template to create your web page, FrontPage Express opens a sample page that you can customize with your own information. If you choose a wizard to walk you through the process of creating a web page, simply answer the questions and click Next to move on to the next series of questions.

Creating and Formatting Text

If you've ever used Microsoft Word, you'll find FrontPage Express very familiar. To add text to your web page, position the cursor where you want to enter new text and then type. To create a new paragraph, press Enter. To format text, select the text and then click the appropriate button or box on the Formatting toolbar (see Figure 10-7).

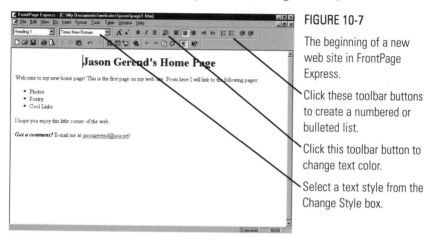

FIGURE 10-7

The beginning of a new web site in FrontPage Express.

Click these toolbar buttons to create a numbered or bulleted list.

Click this toolbar button to change text color.

Select a text style from the Change Style box.

 Text in your web page automatically wraps to a new line. This allows the amount of text per line to change to meet the exact size of your visitors' browser windows.

Inserting and Editing Hyperlinks

Hyperlinks are one of the most important elements on your web site. They link all your pages together and connect your site to the rest of the Internet world. Fortunately, they're easy to create and edit.

To create a hyperlink, highlight the text or image you want your visitors to click and then click the Create Or Edit Hyperlink toolbar button to display the dialog box shown in Figure 10-8.

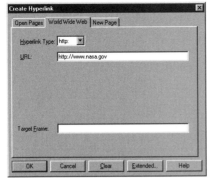

FIGURE 10-8

The Create Hyperlink dialog box is where you create and edit links to other documents and files.

 FrontPage Express automatically creates a hyperlink when you type a URL or e-mail address on a web page.

If you want to create a hyperlink to a web page currently on the Internet, select the type of hyperlink you want to create from the Hyperlink Type box. Most likely you'll select "http:" to indicate you're creating a hyperlink to a web page. You might also want to create an e-mail hyperlink; in this case, select "mailto" from the Hyperlink Type box. After selecting the type of link, enter the URL or address in the URL box and then click OK.

 After you select the Hyperlink Type, FrontPage Express automatically fills out the first part of the URL or address for you, so you don't need to type http:// *or* mailto:.

If you want to link to a page that's already open in FrontPage Express, click the Open Pages tab, select the page you want to link to, and then click OK. To link to a new page that you haven't yet created, click the New Page tab and enter a title for the page in the Page Title box. Enter the future URL for the page in the Page URL box, and then click OK.

To edit a hyperlink, click the hyperlink and then click the Create Or Edit Hyperlink toolbar button. If you want to delete the hyperlink, in the Edit Hyperlink dialog box delete the address in the URL box and then click OK.

Inserting and Editing Horizontal Lines

Horizontal lines have been present on the Web since its inception, and they can really help organize your pages. Insert a horizontal line after a large block of text to visually separate it from what follows. Or add a line underneath your page title to emphasize the title instead of underlining it.

To insert a horizontal line, position the cursor where you want to add the line and then choose the Insert menu's Horizontal Line command. FrontPage Express inserts a horizontal line below your cursor. To edit the line, right-click it and then choose the shortcut menu's Horizontal Line Properties command to display the dialog box shown in Figure 10-9.

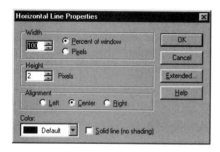

FIGURE 10-9

Use the Horizontal Line Properties dialog box to change the look of your lines.

Inserting Images

Images are part of what makes the Web fun! Although web pages with only text may be practical and useful, adding images to your pages makes them more appealing and attractive for the visitors to your site. Just remember to use discretion with big pictures, or your page will take a long time to load for those people using slow Internet connections.

To add an image to your web page, click the Insert Image toolbar button to display the dialog box shown in Figure 10-10.

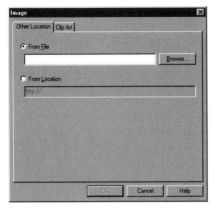

FIGURE 10-10

Use the Image dialog box to tell FrontPage Express where to find the image you want to insert.

Specify the location of your image in the Image dialog box. If the image is on your computer, type the location in the From File box or click Browse to locate it. If the image is on the Internet, click the From Location option button and then enter the URL for the image in the From Location box. If you want to use a piece of clip art, click the Clip Art tab and select an image. Click OK after you've found your image to tell FrontPage Express to insert the image in your page.

Adding Other Elements to Your Web Page

You can use FrontPage Express to add many different items to your web page: tables, background sounds, symbols, comments, and more—many more types of objects than this chapter can cover. However, most of the objects you probably want to create are relatively easy to insert and modify. Just choose the type of object you want to insert from the Insert menu (see Figure 10-11), right-click the object, and then choose the shortcut menu's Properties command to modify the object's settings.

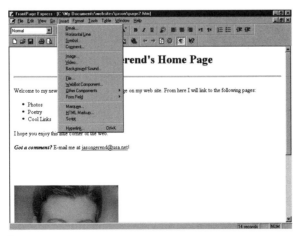

FIGURE 10-11

Use the Insert menu to add to your web page just about any type of object you want.

Saving and Publishing Pages

To save or publish your web page, click the Save toolbar button, type the title you want for your page (this will appear on the title bar in your visitors' browsers), and click As File to save the page to your hard drive (see Figure 10-12).

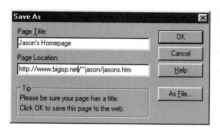

FIGURE 10-12

Enter the title for your page, and specify where you want to save it in the Save As dialog box.

 Notes *If you're familiar with creating your own web pages, you might think this description skips some steps. With FrontPage Express, there is no longer a need to get a separate FTP program to upload your web pages. It's all done automatically as part of the FrontPage Express connection to another program, the Microsoft Web Publishing Wizard.*

If you want to save the page directly to your web site, enter the URL for your site and the filename for your page and then click OK. Unless you have a computer with a special connection on a Local Area **Network**, this usually starts the Web Publishing Wizard. If the Web Publishing Wizard appears, click Next to start the wizard. Fill in any information it requests with the information provided by your web-hosting company, and click Next to proceed to each dialog box.

---

 *The first page on your web site, your **home page**, needs the filename index.htm or index.html in order for your web site to work properly.*

Using Netscape Composer

Netscape Composer is the web-authoring component of Netscape's popular Communicator Internet program. Like FrontPage Express, Netscape Composer is a powerful WYSIWYG tool that is easy to use—and, best of all, it's free. All you need to do to get Netscape Composer is **download** a standard or complete version of Netscape Communicator and install it.

To open Netscape Composer, click the Start button, choose Programs, choose Netscape Communicator, and then click Netscape Composer. Netscape Composer opens up with a blank web page just waiting for your ideas.

Opening Pages

To edit an existing web page, open the page by choosing the File menu's Open Page command and, if the page is on the Internet, entering the **URL** for the page in the box. Click Choose File if the page that you want to open is on your computer (see Figure 10-13).

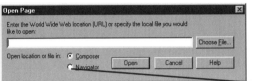

FIGURE 10-13

In the Open Page dialog box, tell Netscape Composer where the page you want to edit is located.

Click this option button to open the page in Netscape Navigator instead of Netscape Composer.

Creating a Page from a Template or Wizard

Netscape Composer doesn't actually come with any templates or a **wizard**, but instead it provides a link to the Netscape web site where a large collection of templates and a very useful web page wizard exist. To create a page from a template or a wizard, choose the File menu's New command and then choose Page From Template or Page From Wizard from the submenu.

To create a page from a template, either enter the URL or path of the page you want to use as a template or click Netscape Templates to use a template from the Netscape web site (see Figure 10-14).

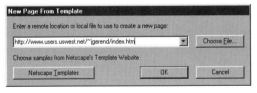

FIGURE 10-14

Use the New Page From Template dialog box to choose a template that you want to base your page on.

To use the wizard to walk through creating your web page, **Netscape Navigator** opens, showing that you're the Netscape Page Wizard (see Figure 10-15).

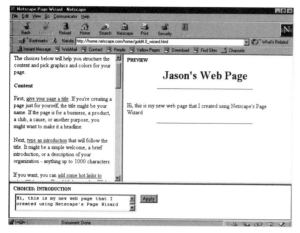

FIGURE 10-15

Click the hyperlinks in the Netscape Page Wizard and then fill out the **form** displayed in the bottom frame to create your page.

The web page is split into three sections, and the Start button is located in the upper right section. If you have a small monitor, you might need to scroll down in this upper right section to see the Start button. Click the Start button to begin, and then click the hyperlinks in the **frame** and fill out the form at the bottom. Click Apply to see your additions in the Preview pane. When you're finished, click Build, and then choose the File menu's Edit Page command to import the page back into Netscape Composer for further editing.

Creating and Formatting Text

You use Netscape Composer to enter text just as you would in any word processor or e-mail program. To add text to your web page, position the cursor where you want to enter the text and then type. To create a new paragraph, press Enter. To check your text for spelling errors, click the Spelling toolbar button. To format your text, select the text and then click the appropriate button or box on the Formatting toolbar (see Figure 10-16).

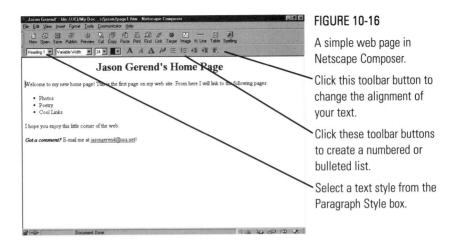

FIGURE 10-16

A simple web page in Netscape Composer.

Click this toolbar button to change the alignment of your text.

Click these toolbar buttons to create a numbered or bulleted list.

Select a text style from the Paragraph Style box.

 Text in your web page automatically wraps to a new line. This allows the amount of text per line to change to meet the exact size of your visitors' browser windows.

Inserting and Editing Hyperlinks

Hyperlinks are one of the most important elements on your web site. Hyperlinks connect your pages to one another and your web site to the rest of the Internet.

To create a hyperlink, highlight the text or image that you want your visitors to click. Then click the Link toolbar button to display the Link tab of the Properties dialog box of your selected element, as shown in Figure 10-17.

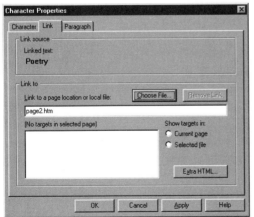

FIGURE 10-17

The Link tab of an object's Properties dialog box is where you create and edit hyperlinks.

To create a hyperlink to a web page or other resource currently on the Internet, enter the URL or address in the Link To A Page Location Or Local File box. If you want to create a link to a page stored on your computer, click Choose File to select the file. Click OK when you're finished.

To edit a hyperlink, click the hyperlink and then click the Link toolbar button. If you want to delete the hyperlink, right-click the hyperlink and then choose the shortcut menu's Remove Link command.

Inserting and Editing Horizontal Lines

Horizontal lines can help you organize the content on your web pages. A horizontal line inserted after a large block of text helps to visually separate it from the elements that follow. Or a line at the top of your page can add emphasis to the title. To insert a horizontal line, position the cursor where you want to add the line and then click the H. Line toolbar button. Netscape Composer inserts a horizontal line below your cursor. To edit the line, double-click it to display the dialog box shown in Figure 10-18.

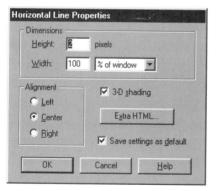

FIGURE 10-18

Use the Horizontal Line Properties dialog box to change the look of your line.

Inserting Images

Images enliven your web pages and give them instant eye appeal for your visitors. But don't go overboard with big pictures because they can take a long time to load.

To add an image to your web page, click the Image toolbar button. Then specify the location of your image in the dialog box shown in Figure 10-19.

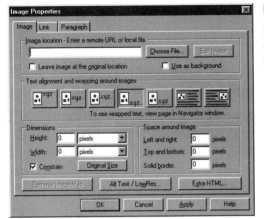

FIGURE 10-19

Use the Image Properties dialog box to tell Netscape Composer where to find the image you want to insert.

If the image is on the Internet, enter the URL for the image in the Image Location box and click OK. If the image is on your computer, click Choose File, locate the file, and then click Open. If you want the image to be a background for your web page, select the Use As Background check box.

Saving and Publishing Pages

To save your web page to your hard drive, click the Save toolbar button, type the filename for your page, and click Save (see Figure 10-20).

FIGURE 10-20

Locate the folder you want to save your page in, and type a filename in the box.

If you want to publish your page to your web site, click the Publish toolbar button to display the dialog box shown in Figure 10-21.

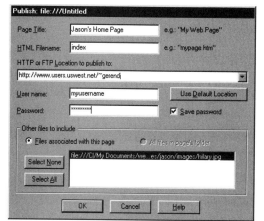

FIGURE 10-21

Fill out all the boxes in the Publish dialog box, and then click OK to save your page to the Web.

Enter the title of your page in the Page Title box. (This title appears at the top of a visitor's browser.) Enter the filename for your page in the HTML Filename box, and then type the URL to which you publish your web pages. (This might be different from the URL you use to view your web site. Ask your web-hosting company for more details.) Enter your user name and **password** in the User Name and Password boxes. The Other Files To Include text box displays a list of files that will be uploaded with the web page. Each of these files is highlighted. If you do not want to upload or publish a file, click it to deselect it. Click OK to upload your files to your web server.

The first page on your web site, your home page, needs the filename index.htm or index.html in order for your web site to work properly.

GLOSSARY

Address Book **Netscape Communicator** and **Microsoft Internet Explorer** both come with an Address Book you can use to store the names and **e-mail** addresses of your contacts. You can also store telephone numbers, street addresses, and other personal information in your Address Book.

AOL Instant Messenger **Netscape Communicator** comes with AOL Instant Messenger, a program you can use to send real-time messages to people.

Attachment An attachment is any file or item that is attached to a message or document but is not actually a part of the document, much as a cover page may be paper-clipped to a document.

Bookmark Just as you might dog-ear an important page in a book, you can bookmark important web pages so that you can easily find them and quickly return to them. Internet Explorer calls bookmarked web pages **Favorites**.

Browser, see **Web browser**

Certificate When you retrieve information from the **Internet**, a certificate issued by an information security company verifies the identity of the source of that information.

Channel A channel is a **web site** that the web site publisher designs with a downloading schedule built in, so when you subscribe, your **web browser** automatically retrieves the web site's content according to the schedule. You can then read the channel content offline. To view a list of channels, click Internet Explorer's Favorites toolbar button and then click the Channels folder.

Chat, see **Microsoft Chat**

Chat room A chat room is an area of the **Internet** where people meet and type comments back and forth to one another in real time.

Client A program that runs on your computer and works in tandem with a **server** program running on another server computer.

Communicator, see **Netscape Communicator**

Composer, see **Netscape Composer**

Connection Wizard, see **Internet Connection Wizard**

Contacts Microsoft Outlook's Contacts folder lets you store contact information for people: their **e-mail** and street addresses, phone numbers, and so forth.

Conversation *Conversation* is the term Outlook and Outlook Express use to describe a group of **newsgroup** or **e-mail** messages that discuss the same subject.

Cookie When you visit a **web site**, the web site's **server** may store a small file called a cookie on your computer to identify you. When you return to the same web site, your **web browser** sends the cookie back to the web server so that it can customize the **web page** for you.

Dial-up networking If you connect to the **Internet** using a **modem** and a telephone line, you use Microsoft Windows' Dial-Up Networking feature to make that connection.

Domain name A domain name is the core part of a **URL** that identifies the owner of the address on the **Internet.**

Download Downloading a file or folder means retrieving a copy of the file or folder from the **Internet** or from a network **server** and saving it locally.

DSL DSL stands for Digital Subscriber Line. A DSL (or ADSL for Asymmetric Digital Subscriber Line) is a fast digital connection to the **Internet.**

E-mail An e-mail message is an electronic message, usually in the form of text, that you send from one computer to another.

Eudora Eudora is a popular **e-mail** client that comes in two versions, a freeware version and a deluxe version. You can obtain Eudora at *http://www.eudora.com.*

FAQ FAQ stands for frequently asked questions. Many **newsgroups** are devoted to FAQs, and many **web sites** include a FAQ page.

Favorites The Favorites folder is a special folder in Internet Explorer that you can use to hold shortcuts to **web pages** and files that you want to be able to find easily. **Netscape Navigator** uses the term *bookmark* to describe these favorite web pages and files.

File extension A file extension is the character sequence (usually three letters long) after the period in a file's name. A file extension indicates a file's type, such as a program file you can run, a text file, or a certain type of image file.

Form Forms are parts of documents or entire documents that contain boxes for people to fill in **online.** Many **web pages** have forms.

Frame A frame is a square or rectangular section of a **web page.** Web pages are often divided into separate rectangular frames that can display information or perform functions. You can select a frame within a web page by clicking it.

FrontPage Express, see Microsoft FrontPage Express

FTP File Transfer Protocol, or FTP, is a set of instructions that lets you move files from one computer to another over the **Internet.** You can browse FTP sites in your **web browser** the way you browse files and folders on your computer.

GIF GIF is a graphic image file format commonly used for small pictures that appear on web pages.

Home page Your home page can refer to the **web page** that your **web browser** displays when you click its Home toolbar button. The term *home page* can also be used to refer to the main web page of any **web site.** So if you've published your own web page or web site on the **World Wide Web,** your home page can refer to this page or to the main page on a multipage web site.

HTML HyperText Markup Language, or HTML, is the standard document format for **web pages** and is an alternate file format for Microsoft Office 2000 documents. HTML is popular because you can apply formatting to HTML documents and the formatting can be viewed almost universally, using a variety of common programs (such as **web browsers**).

HTTP HyperText Transfer Protocol, or HTTP, is the protocol that **clients** and **servers** use to communicate on the **World Wide Web.**

Hyperlink A hyperlink is a block of text or an image that points to another resource (usually on the **Internet**), such as a **web page.**

Internet The Internet is a global **network** of millions of single computers and smaller electronic networks. The Internet lets people across the world share information quickly and inexpensively, which is why the Internet is often referred to as the "Information Superhighway." A couple of the Internet's most popular services are electronic mail (**e-mail**) and the **World Wide Web.**

Internet Connection Wizard The Internet Connection Wizard is a program you can use to set up your **Internet** connection. To use the Connection Wizard, double-click the Connect To The Internet icon on your desktop, or click the Start button, choose Programs, choose Accessories, choose Communications (if available), and then click Internet Connection Wizard. Follow the instructions to set up an Internet connection.

Internet Explorer, see **Microsoft Internet Explorer**

Intranet An intranet is an internal network that works like and uses the technology of the **Internet.**

IP address To access an **Internet** resource, you enter the resource's URL, a name usually made up of letters of the alphabet. But your computer actually locates and identifies resources on the Internet based on a string of numbers and periods called an IP address. For example, to go to the ZDNet **home page,** you can enter *http://www.zdnet.com* in the Address or Location box of your **web browser,** or you can enter 128.11.45.101.

IRC IRC stands for Internet Relay Chat, which is a way of "conversing" with other computer users in real time over the **Internet.**

ISDN Integrated Services Digital Network, or ISDN, is a fast digital connection to the **Internet.** With an ISDN adapter and a special ISDN line from the phone company, you can send and receive information more than twice as fast as with a regular **modem** and phone line.

ISP An Internet service provider, or ISP, is a company that lets you connect your computer to its **network.** Because its network is part of the **Internet,** once you connect to this network, you're connected to the Internet and can use its resources.

Java Java is a programming language frequently used by web publishers because most **web browsers** running on a variety of different **operating systems** can all read the language.

JPEG JPEG is a graphic image file format commonly used for large pictures that appear on web pages and images posted to **newsgroups.**

Kbps Kbps stands for kilobits per second and is a unit for measuring data transfer speed. One kilobit per second is 1,024 bits per second. A bit is the smallest unit of data (either a 0 or a 1).

Link, see **Hyperlink**

Linux   Linux is a version of the UNIX operating system developed by Linus Torvalds of Sweden. Unlike Windows, Linux is freely distributed, complete with its source code (i.e., the program instructions for it).

Log on   You log on (or log in) to a computer to identify yourself. To log on, you enter your user name and **password.** To end a session when you're finished, you log off.

Mbps   Mbps stands for megabits per second and is a unit for measuring data transfer speed. One megabit per second is 1 million bits per second. A bit is the smallest unit of data (either a 0 or a 1).

Microsoft Chat   Microsoft Chat is an Internet Explorer component that allows you to participate in real-time Internet **chat room** discussions.

Microsoft Exchange Server   Exchange Server is a messaging product that corporations frequently use for internal **network** e-mail. Outlook 2000 is specifically designed to work with Exchange Server, providing a number of features that can be used when users send messages to other users across an Exchange Server network.

Microsoft FrontPage Express   FrontPage Express is a mini-version of Microsoft FrontPage that comes with Internet Explorer. You can use FrontPage Express to create and edit **web pages**, but it lacks many of FrontPage's advanced web page– and web site–creation features.

Microsoft Internet Explorer   Internet Explorer is a **web browser** suite that you can use to view **web pages**, search the **Internet**, create and send **e-mail**, access **newsgroups**, video-conference, and chat.

Microsoft NetMeeting   NetMeeting is a conferencing program that you can use to share programs, collaborate on documents, draw on a whiteboard, chat using the keyboard, or meet with a group of people using audio or video.

Microsoft Outlook   Outlook is a personal information manager that you can use to send and receive **e-mail**, manage tasks, keep an appointment calendar, and maintain an address book.

Microsoft Outlook Express   Outlook Express is a mini-version of Outlook that you can use to send and receive **e-mail** and create and maintain an **address book**. Outlook Express also lets you work with **newsgroups** and functions as Outlook's newsreader.

Microsoft Windows Windows is a family of **operating systems** that grew out of the original Windows program that ran on top of Microsoft's DOS operating system. The Windows family includes the now-discontinued Windows 3.1, and Windows 95, Windows 98, Windows 2000, Windows CE, and Windows NT.

Modem A modem is a device that allows you to connect your computer to a telephone line so that you can send and receive information from other computers on a local **network** or on the **Internet**.

NetMeeting, see **Microsoft NetMeeting**

Netscape Communicator Netscape Communicator is a free **suite** of **Internet** programs that includes **AOL Instant Messenger, Netscape Composer, Netscape Messenger,** and **Netscape Navigator.**

Netscape Composer Netscape Composer is a program that helps you create and publish **web pages.**

Netscape Messenger Netscape Messenger is a program that allows you to send and receive **e-mail** and post and read **newsgroup** messages.

Netscape Navigator Netscape Navigator is a **web browser.** You can use it to view **web pages** and search the **Internet** for information.

Network A network is a group of computers that are connected together so that the computer users can share information and resources.

Newsgroup A newsgroup is a collection of messages—typically text messages—that people post to a central **server** so that other people may read them. Newsgroup messages closely resemble **e-mail** messages—in fact, you use the same basic process to create and post a newsgroup message as you do to create and send an e-mail message.

Newsgroup reader A newsgroup reader, or newsreader, is any program that allows you to read and write messages on a **newsgroup.** **Outlook Express** is the newsgroup reader that comes with **Internet Explorer,** Office, and **Windows.**

Online Working online (as opposed to working offline) means that your **Internet** (or **network**) connection is open and ready for use.

Online service An online service is an **ISP** that also provides or organizes content for its customers. For example, an online service might provide its own software and private **newsgroups** and **chat rooms** for its customers. An example of an online service is America Online (AOL).

Operating system An operating system (OS) is the software on your computer that manages your computer's hardware and resources. **Microsoft Windows** 95, Windows 98, Windows 2000, and Windows NT are all operating systems, as are **Linux** and the Mac OS. Programs are designed to work with particular operating systems.

Outlook, see **Microsoft Outlook**

Outlook Express, see **Microsoft Outlook Express**

Password A password is a secret word or string of characters that you use to confirm your identity.

POP POP stands for Post Office Protocol and is a standard protocol used for receiving **e-mail.**

Relative URL A relative URL describes where a file is in reference to the current **web page.** For example, if the file is in the same directory as the web page containing the link, the relative URL is the same as the filename, such as FILE.JPG. If the file is in a subdirectory called IMAGES, then the relative URL is the filename plus the path to the subdirectory, or /IMAGES/FILE.JPG. Relative URLs are useful because they don't break apart when you move your web pages; as long as the pages are in the same directories relative to one another, the **hyperlinks** work whether the files are on your hard drive or on the **Internet.**

Search engine A search engine, also called a search service, allows you to search the **Internet** either by entering a keyword or by browsing resources by category. Popular search engines include AltaVista, HotBot, and Yahoo!

Server A server on the **Internet** is a computer that people log onto or visit to view **web pages** or **download** e-mail messages and files, among other things. For example, the computer that does the work of delivering the **e-mail** messages you send, or retrieving and storing the messages that people send you, is called a mail server. A news server holds **newsgroups** that you can browse and post messages to.

Shareware Shareware is software that you are encouraged to try out for a period of time and share with others for free. You must pay for it if you decide to keep it.

SMTP The Simple Mail Transfer Protocol (SMTP) is a common protocol used for sending **e-mail** messages over the **Internet.**

Spam Spam is unsolicited bulk **e-mail** you receive (the electronic equivalent of junk mail). Spam messages are most often advertisements. The term *spam* can also apply to **newsgroup** messages posted to numerous newsgroups and usually not related to the focus of the newsgroup.

Stationery You can apply **HTML** stationery to add pizzazz to the look of **e-mail** messages created with **Outlook** or **Outlook Express**, just as you use pre-printed paper stationery to make a hand-written letter look nicer.

Suite A suite is a set of software programs offered in a single package.

Synchronize You use Internet Explorer's Synchronize command to download the latest version of any offline pages you have set up, as well as changes to any web folders you set up for offline viewing.

T1 line A T1 line is a high-bandwidth digital telephone line often used by larger businesses and organizations to make high-speed connections to the **Internet.**

Telnet The Windows Telnet accessory allows you to connect to Telnet **servers** and browse text. If your local library system isn't yet on the **World Wide Web,** you may be able to browse the catalog using Telnet.

Thread *Thread* is the term that **Netscape Messenger** uses to describe a group of **e-mail** or **newsgroup** messages that discuss the same subject.

URL URL stands for uniform resource locator. A URL is an address for an **Internet** location.

Usenet Usenet is a worldwide **network**, consisting mainly of UNIX machines, that hosts tens of thousands of **newsgroups** devoted to various topics.

vCard A vCard is the electronic equivalent of a business card. It contains your contact information and can be attached to an **e-mail** message for the recipient to copy.

Virus A computer virus is a program that a malicious person creates to impair the functioning of some part of your computer. It is easy to catch a virus by downloading infected files from the **World Wide Web** or by opening infected e-mail **attachments**, so you should save or open such files only from trustworthy sources. An antivirus program checks files for viruses.

Web browser A web browser is a program that lets you view **web pages** on the **World Wide Web.** Popular web browsers include **Microsoft Internet Explorer** and **Netscape Navigator.**

Web page A web page is a file that a business or individual publishes to the **World Wide Web** for other people to see. Web pages commonly include multimedia elements—such as pictures, text, and even sound. They generally include **hyperlinks** connecting them to other web pages.

Web site A web site is a collection of **web pages** connected by **hyperlinks.** People and companies publish web sites on the **World Wide Web** when they have more information to share than will fit comfortably on one page. For example, a company web site might include one web page listing products and services, one listing employment opportunities, one with hyperlinks to the latest news releases, and so on.

WebTV WebTV is a product and service that lets you browse the **World Wide Web** and use e-mail with your television.

Wildcard When you search for a file, a block of text, or even a resource on the **Internet,** you can often use a wildcard to take the place of one or more other characters. The most common wildcard is the asterisk (*).

Windows, see **Microsoft Windows**

Wizard A wizard is a little program that steps you through a process by asking questions. It collects your answers and then produces, for example, a **web page** or a fax cover sheet.

World Wide Web The World Wide Web (WWW), or the Web for short, is the collection of **web pages** on the **Internet** that are interconnected by **hyperlinks.**

Zip To zip a file means to compress it using a utility such as WinZip, EasyZip, or PKzip so that the file shrinks in size for easier transport.

INDEX

INDEX

INDEX

This book was prepared and submitted to Barnes & Noble Books in electronic form. The manuscript was written using Microsoft Word 2000. Pages were composed using PageMaker 6.5 for Windows.

Interior Text Designer
Stefan Knorr

Writers
Kaarin Dolliver, Jason Gerend & Steve Nelson

Editor
Paula Thurman

Technical Editor
Michael Jang

Indexer
Julie Kawabata

Proofreader
Jay Cotten